Curves of Steel

STREAMLINED AUTOMOBILE DESIGN
AT PHOENIX ART MUSEUM

Curves of Steel

STREAMLINED AUTOMOBILE DESIGN
AT PHOENIX ART MUSEUM

EDITED BY JONATHAN A. STEIN
PHOTOGRAPHS BY MICHAEL FURMAN
EXHIBIT CURATOR DENNITA SEWELL

TABLE OF CONTENTS

INTRODUCTION

Design is often for the sake of beauty and, other times, it is purely for function. But there is a certain joy and pleasure to be had from that which is both beautiful and fills a need. A fine watch is both a lovely piece of craftsmanship and an essential tool, while a Chippendale chest is a pleasure to behold as well as a convenient place to store clothing.

Rarely do the worlds of art and technology meet as successfully as they have in the finest examples of the automobile. In the beginning, automobiles were only nominally functional. They were cantankerous contraptions best suited as the toys of the wealthy. In appearance, they were clearly evolved from horse-drawn carriages and coaches. First came the mechanical improvements that allowed them to become reliable transportation. Eventually, the styling moved away from the horse-age model and became less upright and more modern.

The Curves of Steel exhibit celebrates the automobile's graduation into the modern age. None of the cars in this wonderfully diverse display show even a passing connection to their horse-powered antecedents. But, unlike prior mainstream museum exhibits such as the Museum of Modern Art's Celebrated Eight Automobiles of 1951, this display is not about the automobile purely as a pleasing assemblage of angles and curves. It is a demonstration of how the automobile grew up and gained an aesthetic purpose that allowed it to become a more efficient tool of transportation. Thanks to the expansive galleries of the Phoenix Art Museum, there is room to assemble and display twenty-two large rolling expressions of the convergence of art and science.

What could be more efficient than a streamlined people mover that offers utility, beauty and an air-splitting shape as it moves five or six people in comfort? The term "people mover" may evoke the image of a modern minivan, but in this context it refers to the stunning Art Deco Stout Scarab that adorns the main entry way of Phoenix Art Museum. The Lincoln Zephyr is no less extraordinary in that it combined the benefits of aerodynamic design with undeniable elegance in a way that appealed to thousands of American motorists. Both were distinctly American versions of large cars intended to radically revise the public's view of the automobile.

Enter the main gallery and you'll be struck by the Czech Tatra T87. Although this example dates from 1948, the rear-engined, fully-streamlined auto-mobile was revolutionary when it debuted in 1936. Engineered by Hans Ledwinka and employing the design concepts of pioneering aerodynamicist Paul Jaray, it was the first thoroughly modern aero-dynamically-designed automobile to see series production. With a short nose, flat sides, skirted wheels and a sloping roofline topped by a dorsal fin, there was nothing on the road like the Tatra.

In France, Jean Andreau's pioneering aerodynamic work was responsible for what is arguably the most dramatic statement of streamline design — the Dubonnet Xenia. Contemporary designs by other French designers and coachbuilders placed less emphasis on pure aerodynamic theory as they pursued beauty with determination. Jean Bugatti's fabulous Atlantic coupé, Pourtout's Delage, and Figoni's Darracq and Delahaye cabriolets, as well as his show-stopping Talbot-Lago Teardrop coupé must be considered the high watermark of all automotive design. These examples of rolling art cut through the air with less wind resistance than most of their contemporaries. They are unquestioned objects of beauty that combine fluid form and illustrate that, while aerodynamics were hardly forgotten, the craftsman responsible for these masterpieces valued art above all else.

The other vehicles on display emphasize art or technology in varying proportions. The sleek

STREAMLINED EIGHT-CYLINDER PASSENGER CAR WITH AIR COOLED REAR-ENGINE 100 miles/h

The Tatra T87 combined the work of aerodynamic pioneer Paul Jaray and engineer Hans Ledwinka. This period rendering shows the similarity between the shape of airships and the T87, which isn't surprising considering that Jaray started his career designing Zeppelin airships.

Ferrari TRC and the Alfa Romeo 8C-2900B were styled more by eye than by wind-tunnel. However, both the Darl'mat Peugeot and the Embiricos Bentley combined the art of Pourtout and the considerable aerodynamic design skills of Georges Poulin.

Never before have so many four-wheeled objets d'art, showcasing the evolution of the art of aero-dynamics and streamlining, been assembled under one roof. From French extravaganza to designer Gordon Buehrig's futuristic Cord and on to the startling innovation of the So-Cal Special dry lakes racer and the 200 mph hour luxury of the McLaren F1, Curves of Steel tells the tale of how art and science joined to shape man's mobility in the 20th century.

— Jonathan A. Stein

7

Paul Jaray's pioneering aerodynamic designs were executed (from left to right) Tatra T-77, Fiat Balilla, Maybach SW-35 and Audi.

PREFACE

"Slippery." "Cheat the Wind." "Form Follows Function." Such terms evolved as stylists put little ribbons on their wind-tunnel mock-ups.

The concept of curved coachwork began in the earliest days of racing. Typical examples, all in the very beginning of the last century, included Stanley's speed record Steamer, Winton's Bullet and Jenatzy's Jamais Contende. Remarkably, curves did not appear outside of competition until the late 1920s with the exception of some quirks such as Germany's dumpy Rumpler and Count Ricotti's ALFA Fantasy.

The dark ages of automobile design did lighten when speedsters appeared, characterized by rounded boat tails. Designers soon realized that a curvaceous rear end could attract discerning gentlemen and perhaps sell cars. Auburn's Speedster is the ultimate example of the idiom.

Although theoreticists such as Paul Jaray and Jean Andreau proffered curves for reducing wind resistance, curves became common because they were sexier—not because they were slipperier. They were *de rigeur* in the 1930s, finally, as evidenced by the oldest car in this collection, a 1934 Chrysler Imperial Airflow.

Chrysler's bulbous Airflow and the appropriately-named Stout set a standard which was not cured until the late 1930s, when Italian and French artists put curves on a diet, adding aesthetics to perceived aerodynamic efficiencies.

The 1940s were heralded by the soap bar curves of the Chrysler Thunderbolt, but saved somewhat by the Tucker, and Tatra's persistent efforts to create a new streamliner virtually every year.

By the 1950s, curves sold sports-racing cars such as the Testa Rossa and found their way into representative models of many manufacturers.

The authors have chosen and magnificently displayed their candidates for the archetypical Curves of Steel. The reader will be amazed at man's desire to create automotive beauty and photographer Michael Furman's ability to bring it to life.

— Frederick A. Simeone, M.D.

THE ORIGINS OF AUTOMOTIVE STREAMLINING

As applied to the automobile, the word "streamlined" implies a vehicle designed to slip through the air with efficiency. Throughout the history of the automobile, inspiration for streamlining cars has come from different sources. Many cars have been designed with a genuine attempt to incorporate contemporary knowledge of aerodynamics. Just as many cars have been styled to merely appear aerodynamically efficient, and there have also been many cars that were never conceived to be streamlined at all.

At the dawn of the car industry, the speeds attained by automobiles did not warrant the application of aerodynamic principles, which were still relatively undeveloped; thoughts of flying machines were still just thoughts. However, in 1899, Camille Jenatzy built a record-breaking electric car that had a body shape very reminiscent of the simultaneously developed Zeppelin airship. Although it achieved a speed of 62 mph, it's doubtful whether the body shape contributed anything significant to its aerodynamic properties, particularly as the exposed wheels and axles would have negated any small advantage derived from the body shape. But it did show that some people were already thinking about how an object carves through the air. By the time cars were approaching speeds where aerodynamic efficiency would have some modest benefit, early aircraft and airships were a reality. This inspired the application of more sophisticated aeronautical knowledge to cars.

In Europe, several auto engineers and designers experimented with applying functional aerodynamics to cars. Aerodynamicists had already determined that the tear-drop was the optimum aerodynamic form and early work on submersibles and airships bore this out. A classic early example of a tear-drop shaped car was the Count Ricotti-designed and Castagna-bodied ALFA of 1913. While somewhat more advanced than the Jenatzy creation, it still failed to take into account the disruptive influence of the open wheels and untidy under-chassis.

As always, wars accelerate technological progress and so, by the end of World War I, a good deal more was known about aircraft aerodynamics, in Europe and the United States. Some of this new know-how began to be experimentally applied to cars.

During the next decade, more scientifically sound, aerodynamic cars were proposed by pioneers in the field such as A. Riedler, Ludwig Prandtl, Gustave Eiffel, Edmund Rumpler and, a little later, the likes of Paul Jaray, Hans Ledwinka and Wunibald Kamm.

Rumpler's Tropfenwagen of 1921 actually had a better coefficient of drag than the best of today's production cars. Much of this wave of activity was centered around Czechoslovakia and Germany, which were both at the forefront of automotive technology between the wars. However, speeds of most road vehicles at the time still did not require much in the way of aerodynamic efficiency. Most of the streamlined cars that were prototyped or put into production by the likes of Kamm, Jaray and Adler were larger, more luxurious cars, cars like Hans Ledwinka's Tatra Type 87 produced in Czechoslovakia. Smaller German and Czech cars of the 1930s certainly made some reference to aerodynamic principles, the Volkswagen Beetle being a good example.

Meanwhile, in the United States, after the First World War, commercial air travel started to flourish at perhaps a greater rate than in Europe. Clean and aerodynamically efficient forms developed

Above: Count Ricotti commissioned Castagna to create this experimental body on an ALFA 40-60 chassis in 1914.

As this Rumpler advertisement illustrates so graphically, Edmund Rumpler's streamlined designs were far ahead of those being used by contemporary automakers.

quite quickly as the aircraft industry proliferated, culminating in aviation icons such as the Douglas Dakota DC3. In the public's mind, these aerodynamic forms began to replace the classic ocean liner's visual identity that had been an iconic form of technical progress while evoking the romanticism of glamorous travel.

NORMAN BEL GEDDES

It was not long before industrial designers began to be influenced by the more aerodynamic, aviation look as they applied their influence to manufactured consumer goods including locomotives, complete trains, buses and trucks. In the 1930s, this taste for streamlining included many static manufactured products too, such as pencil sharpeners, radios, office equipment and buildings. Of course, these objects and buildings did not need to be aerodynamic, but many designers and consumers were attracted to the simple, clean and often elegant forms that they displayed.

Raymond Loewy and Norman Bel Geddes were notable industrial designers who emphasized streamlined forms in static products that they created. They were also commissioned to design a few cars, which helped influence the car industry at large to follow suit in pursuing the streamlined form. In both Europe and America, cars were introduced that appeared to be aerodynamic due to their curvaceous and often sensual forms. This contrasted with the architectural and rectilinear cars that had been the norm. Such cars were the 1934 Chrysler Airflow and the Lincoln Zephyr. While the intent of these cars was clear, it is doubtful whether their aerodynamic efficiency was significantly better than regular cars of the time. The Chrysler was the first such car seen by Americans and was deemed too radical. Its sales were very disappointing so, by 1937, the car was

discontinued. The later Lincoln Zephyr, although undoubtedly inspired by the Airflow, faired better, hitting the market when the public had become more familiar with such automotive looks.

Meanwhile, in Europe, French coachbuilders were responsible for some of the most flamboyantly designed cars ever seen, notably the teardrop coupés of Figoni & Falaschi or the Dubonnet Xenia by Saoutchik. This extraordinary genre of cars represented the zenith of the streamlining art; they were more an expression of art than rigorous aerodynamic study.

The Second World War again punctuated automobile design development. Inevitably, the exponential advance in militarily driven technology, on all sides, had the effect of accelerating the rate of change in car shapes in the years that followed. The aftermath of this second global conflict brought with it a public awareness of rockets, the dawn of jet fighters and the prospect of space travel.

In the United States, the post WWII years brought a sense of economic and cultural optimism that primed the public to expect more flamboyant looking automobiles. American auto manufacturers, with design studios staffed by a generation of designers who had just witnessed tumultuous events, obliged this expectation by seducing the public with fantastic dream cars that were overtly influenced by jet fighters and the nascent space race. These show cars were generously adorned with air intakes and nacelles that any aeronautical engineer would have been proud of, along with a surfeit of fins and contours that shouted "airplane." It is probably fair to say that never before or since has the car industry teased the public with such a hyped vision of the future.

Apparently the public applauded because, during the latter half of the fifties, America saw more and more dramatically styled production cars from all the major Detroit manufacturers. The famous

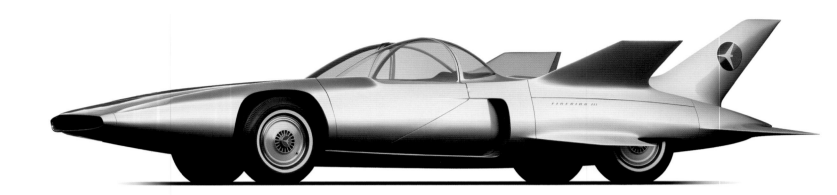

chrome, fins and rocket ship era of American automobile design reached its peak around the 1960 model year when the largest fins, the most ornate protuberances and outrageously excessive, gratuitous decoration appeared almost universally. While obviously inspired by the "hi-tech" aerospace industry of the time, suffice to say, few if any of these cars possessed any aerodynamic integrity or advantage; it was all style.

In Europe it was different. Economically stricken as a result of the hostilities, the public and the car industry had very different priorities to their American counterparts. Efficiency was the name of the game. Most of the European car companies resumed production of either their prewar models or hastily contrived new models on a tight budget. However, leading automobile designers and engineers were very conscious of the aerospace developments and some considerable

research went into automobile aerodynamics, but more with a view to improving fuel consumption than to titillate the public. The B.A.T series of concept vehicles by the Italian design house Bertone, despite their audacity, were genuinely well-researched cars that did influence some subsequent production cars.

Despite financial hardships, the Europeans were enthusiastic to get back to their beloved motor racing and, in the 1950s, many racing cars benefited from courageous aerodynamic experimentation. This certainly influenced the design and shape of road cars, particularly the more performance-oriented vehicles. Much of this aerodynamic endeavor was a little naïve but it was well intentioned, and the quest for fuel efficiency saw significant advances through the 1960s and 1970s. American ideas about streamlining, postwar, had only a modest influence on European car design.

The first energy crisis of the mid-1970s became a major catalyst for aerodynamic progress on both sides of the Atlantic. During the late 1970s, aerodynamic studies by the world's car companies became much more scientific and, while still light years away from the aircraft industry, genuine progress was made. Suddenly a rash of production cars appeared that had significantly lower coefficients of drag, cars such as the Audi 100 (Germany), the Ford Sierra (Germany/UK) and the Ford Taurus (US). Not only were the drag coefficients lower, but also, a significantly better understanding of cross-wind stability, wind noise and engine cooling characteristics brought benefits to their buyers. These cars were aerodynamically improved through careful attention to detail: flush-fitting windows, studied control of contours and smoother undersides, rather than blatant teardrop forms.

Since the 1980s, when every car advertisement boasted of a low aerodynamic drag, the marketing focus on streamlining has disappeared but, in fact, all of the car manufacturers have been steadily working away on genuinely improving the aerodynamic performance of everyday cars. The irony is that cars no longer need to look particularly streamlined to actually be aero-efficient, such is the intrinsic knowledge of the subject.

However, there is still huge opportunity for a more radical approach to shaping cars for energy efficiency. As we now enter a new energy chapter, a radical shift in the supply and demand equation will likely drive a new and zealous bout of making cars that truly cleave the air with minimum effort.

– Geoff Wardle

Opposite: In the late 1940s and throughout the 1950s and early 1960s, General Motors explored spaceage themes with the 1959 Firebird III, and the 1959 Cadillac Eldorado.

Above: The Bristol 401, incorporated themes carried over from the pre-war BMWs as well as Bristol's aircraft experience and extensive input from the masters as Touring in Milan.

AMERICAN STREAMLINED CARS

STREAMLINE AMERICA

In ancient Greece, Zephyr was the name of the god of the west wind. In 1930s America, Zephyr was the name of a passenger train, a model of electric clock, and a clever office address gadget, later called the Rolodex. Most famously, Zephyr was the name of the Lincoln automobile that the Museum of Modern Art would call the first successful streamlined passenger car.

The name perfectly summed up the modern mythology of the streamlining movement— romantic, high flown and a bit grandiose. Streamlining aimed to make objects move through the air with the least drag possible and was built on the conviction that the most efficient form must also be the most beautiful—a sentiment that went back to the builders of clipper ships and fast yachts. "If it looks right, it will work right," was a romantic ideal.

RAYMOND LOEWY

Streamlining helped produce a tradition of automobiles that were works of high style, great art, and cultural power. But it was also a wider movement that shaped product design, architecture and graphics and, in the 1930s, enjoyed the prestige held today by digital technology. It symbolized progress, faith in the constant benefits of technology, and a delight in the increasing speed and excitement of life. Zephyr's wind was the wind of change.

In the United States, streamlining came less from the wind tunnel than from style and sales. As the Zephyr name suggests, objects that didn't move were streamlined at the same time or even sooner than ones that actually did—like automobiles. Streamlined irons and vacuum cleaners promised speedier completion of housework.

Streamlining was a popular culture, like Hollywood films. The automobile's streamlining implied individual opportunity. In the car, social and economic mobility were symbolized by physical mobility—an economy that provided automobile ownership not just to the very wealthy but to most Americans. Streamlining was also sold as an antidote to the Depression—a way to speed sales in the face of economic drag. The resistance most streamlined products were styled to overcome was sales resistance. "He streamlines the sales curve" trumpeted *Time* magazine when it put designer Raymond Loewy on its cover.

Other industrial designers, such as Henry Dreyfuss and Norman Bel Geddes, applied a common approach to all kinds of objects, from appliances to gas stations and ocean liners. They showed objects evolving toward an ever sleeker future. "MAYA" was the acronym Loewy coined—"most advanced, yet acceptable." Widely reproduced images by Bel Geddes popularized the ideal of a future automobile shaped like the iconic teardrop on skirted wheels. A more refined version of this fantasy was used in Bel Geddes' depiction of future highways at General Motors' Futurama Pavilion at the 1939 World's Fair in New York.

Opposite page: The Airflow and General Motors' new streamlined passenger trains for the Union Pacific Railroad were symbols of new design directions.

But actual auto production was different. Before the 1930s, automobile construction still combined wood and metal crafts. The move to stamping out body panels of sheet steel militated toward curved shapes that lent themselves to stamping dies. Even luxury cars changed from custom or tailor made products to mass produced ones. In the terms of the apparel industry they changed from *couture to pret a porter.*

Streamlining capitalized on the fascination with aviation in the wake of Lindbergh's crossing of the Atlantic and the arrival of modern airliners such as the DC-3.

The Lincoln Zephyr was photographed beside the Burlington Zephyr streamlined locomotive and also with Amelia Earhart and

her record setting Lockheed Electra airplane. But streamlined shapes also proclaimed their affinity to nature and the forms of bird and fish, shaped by the laws of fluid dynamics.

It was almost forty years after the invention of the automobile before manufacturers made serious efforts to shape its form to reduce drag. In part, this reflected speeds that remained for the most part below 50 mph. But it also spoke of the coach building heritage of the body builders. Before any ambitions to create an overall streamline form, what designer and historian Strother McMinn called "a coherent carefully sculptured shell," a few innovators sought to round fenders

and bodies—for grace as much as efficiency. Often, these were for smaller companies struggling to stand out. The flowing lines of the Reo Royale of 1931—frequently referred to as the first streamlined production car—the Graham Blue Streak and other models he designed earned Amos Northrop praise as "the Mozart of auto design."

Other early ideas for streamlined vehicles were visionary if not downright eccentric—like the Scarab, produced by the colorful William Stout and Buckminster Fuller's Dymaxion car, shown at the 1933 Century of Progress Exhibition in Chicago.

The Lincoln Zephyr evolved from another car seen at the Century of Progress, the Briggs Dream Car, which was based on the designs of John Tjaarda. That car impressed Edsel Ford, who acquired the design. With minor styling changes and the engine moved to its conventional spot up front, the car was introduced as the Lincoln Zephyr in 1936. Its graceful body lines dramatically contrasted with the ungainly mustache-like front of the Airflow. The Zephyr was a popular success. Even iconic architect Frank Lloyd Wright bought one.

The twin inspirations for streamlining, aviation and nature, were invoked in selling the Zephyr. "It's the next best thing to flying," the advertising intoned. "You are skimming straight for the horizon...

watch out or you will bump into one of those billowy clouds." Another ad showed the Zephyr beside a leaping sailfish with the phrase "naturally streamlined."

The popular and aesthetic success of the Zephyr stood in contrast to the aesthetic challenge of the 1934 Chrysler Airflow, which made an appearance in Chicago the second year of the fair. There was a lesson in the difference.

Although Walter Chrysler signed up Norman Bel Geddes as a consultant, the design of the Airflow was put largely in the hands of the engineers, led by Carl Breer. The Airflow received huge publicity. It was depicted as revolutionary. "For him the buggy is bugaboo!" proclaimed the editors of *Time* magazine in a cover story on Walter Chrysler. The rounded Airflow adopted the rough shape of Paul Jaray's patented aerodynamic shape and was sold for its benefits in reducing drag: "It bores through the air!" (Indeed, Jaray's American office successfully sued Chrysler for patent royalties.) But the Airflow was plagued with production and quality problems. For all the excitement, the car's appearance put off many buyers. Only 55,000 of the model's variants were sold over four years of production, despite cosmetic improvements. When he wrote his autobiography a few years later, Walter Chrysler never mentioned the car.

By the mid 1930s, the word "streamlined" was everywhere in automobile advertising.

Although Cadillac offered a model called the aerodynamic coupe at the Century of Progress, General Motors resisted the fascination with streamlining. Only at the end of the 1930s did streamlining arrive at GM, as the so-called torpedo look. Under Harley Earl, rather than adopting the overall teardrop or Jaray body shape, designers produced a vocabulary of "streamlined" shapes and graphic elements, such as fenders and headlights and chromed accents. The Pontiac "Silver Streak" look created by Frank Hershey employed parallel chrome "speedlines" that industrial designers had equated with speed and progress.

By 1940, the extreme claims of streamlining began to meet with skepticism. Cartoons mocked streamlined appliances and the Museum of Modern Art condemned the streamlined toaster. Hollywood borrowed the 1938 Phantom Corsair for the film comedy "Young at Heart," derisively renaming it "The Flying Wombat."

And World War II soon made a mockery of the more romantic and hopeful depictions of technology and design as the means to a happy future for all.

The postwar vocabulary of fins and propeller spinners, inspired by fighter planes, saw a shift to less subtle, symbolic allusion. The excesses of 1950s designs, with rocket inspired fins and jet nacelle grilles, reached baroque extremes. Not until the 1986 Ford Taurus did a Detroit manufacturer again evoke streamlining with claims for "aero design" as a source of fuel economy as well as style. But great designs like the Zephyr, the Cord 810 and Auburn 851 transcended and outlasted 1930s fashions. The ideal of a streamlined shape combining utility and beauty persisted. No one explained its lure better than Ferdinand Porsche, who argued that shapes built on the timeless laws of physics will always appeal because they satisfy a deep human desire—the desire for immortality.

– Phil Patton

Opposite page: The Lincoln Zephyr was a startlingly clean and sleek design that, unlike the Chrysler Airflow, proved that aerodynamic automobile shapes could be beautiful.

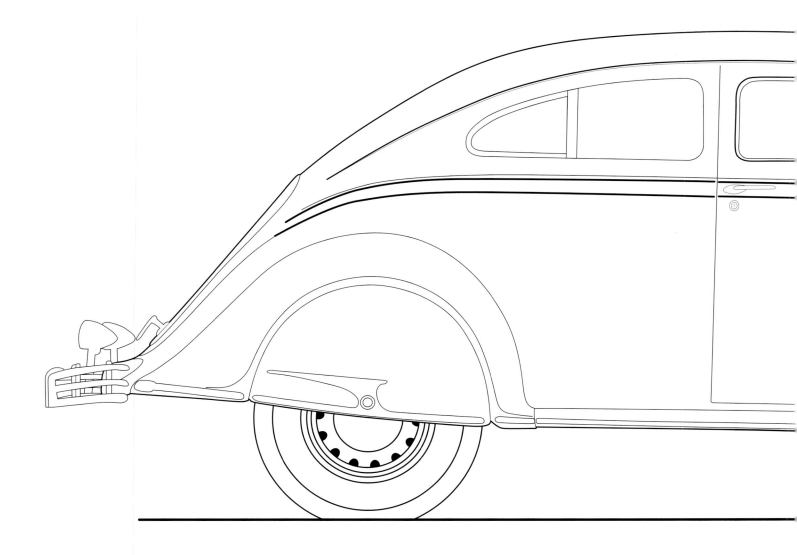

1934 CHRYSLER AIRFLOW IMPERIAL

The first Chrysler Airflow Imperial this writer ever saw was in Carl Breer's garage. It took my breath away. Photographs hadn't prepared me for the majestic size of the car, its voluble presence, its dramatic statement.

That the inspiration for the Airflow came from Breer's mistaking a squadron of airplanes for a flock of geese has been iterated so often as to sound apocryphal. But it did happen on a summer's family drive to Port Huron in 1927, and set Breer to thinking about the struggle a plane has pushing itself through the air, and the effect this air resistance has on automobiles.

Back in his office at Highland Park, Breer asked William Earnshaw to investigate the problem. A recent addition to the Chrysler engineering staff from Dayton, Ohio, Earnshaw asked Orville Wright, and Wright said a wind tunnel was needed. One was immediately built in Dayton, subsequently a larger one in Highland Park. "We pioneered by not wasting time," Breer said.

To his astonishment and that of his crew, the wind tunnel demonstrated contemporary production cars were 30 percent more efficient conquering wind resistance when driven backwards. "Just think how dumb we have been," Breer observed

looking at the parking lot from the window of Chrysler's fourth floor engineering lab. "All those cars have been running in the wrong direction."

Moving the bulk of an automobile from the back to the front was the logical first step, which meant relocating the rear seat from over the rear axle to ahead of it, with all other chassis components moving forward as well. Moving ahead, too, was the engine, to a position *over* rather than *behind* the front axle, with engine and transmission tilted down slightly to lower the driveshaft. This, in turn, lowered the car's center of gravity and the floor of the passenger compartment.

Contemporary American automobiles bolted wood-framed metal bodies to heavy steel chassis frames. The Breer team chose a "bridge truss"

(in the company's phrase) that was, in essence, a metal cage adding strength to the entire vehicle. What the wind tunnel had told to Chrysler engineers would result in an automobile of extraordinary handling and riding qualities.

Styling chief Oliver Clark worked with Breer on body contours that seemed to happen naturally. Elimination of the removable hood sides extended the body forward, allowing for a wide windshield. "Oliver Clark and I decided that a flat windshield of this magnitude would look terrible," Breer said. Curved would be far better. Doing away with the windshield's center division post was another good idea. Pittsburgh Glass research engineer Herb Sherts may have gulped when asked to make such a difficult piece of glass, but he succeeded in doing it.

CARL
BREER

A half decade after Carl Breer's failure to identify aircraft in formation, the first prototype was completed. Automakers seldom tested new cars on streets in the Detroit area, and it was out of the question for this remarkably different automobile. For secrecy, the car was trucked to a large farm outside Detroit. Just a few miles on the road told the story. "Most astonishing was the relaxed feeling that came from the ride," Carl Breer said. "It was a great day." Walter Chrysler was asked to spend an afternoon at the farm, which he did some time later, and enthusiastically gave the go-ahead.

Production plans brought compromise as cost factors decreed the one-piece curved windshield be assigned only to the top-of-the-line Imperial and not the Chrysler or DeSoto versions of the car that virtually named itself Airflow. The Airflow was introduced at the New York National Automobile Show in January 1934 to celebrate Chrysler's tenth anniversary, and the car was very well received. Thousands of orders were taken. Subsequent advertising ballyhooed a car "That Literally Bores a Hole through the Air" and allowed lucky owners to "Read a Newspaper at 80 Miles an Hour on a Dirt Road."

Glitches delayed deliveries until April, and the rush to get the Airflow off the assembly line brought glitches in the cars themselves. This was a situation scarcely unique to the Airflow, but one that Carl Breer wholly blamed for the disappointing sales of the car. One might say he was in a bit of denial. "Fashioned by Function" was the headline of early ads. Mass America did not find the Airflow fashionable. To many, it resembled one's homely eccentric great aunt. The car was too avant-garde for all save the discerning and those who didn't care what a car looked like so long as they could read the Wall Street Journal at speed on rough roads.

Moreover, General Motors, alarmed that the Airflow might steal the thunder from GM's mildly streamlined lineup, launched an anti-Airflow campaign, extolling its own efforts as the "product of deliberate growth rather than abrupt inspiration" and lambasting the Airflow as an "ill-timed" and "dubious" experiment.

The confluence of these factors weighed heavy on the Airflow. To counteract, Chrysler sent the car racing (Harry Hartz set 72 AAA records at Bonneville) across the continent (for an economy record of 18.1 mph), and pushed a driver-less car over a 110-foot Pennsylvania cliff to tumble end-over-end and land on its wheels at the bottom, whereon a driver opened the door, got in and motored away.

Undoing the Breer/Clark body styling, most especially the compound-curve waterfall grille, was the assignment given industrial designer Norman Bel Geddes mid-1934, and to new Chrysler design chief Ray Dietrich for '35, '36 and '37. The new visage did not reverse the Airflow's fortunes and the model was unceremoniously dropped after 1937. "Although the Airflow as a total vehicle did not succeed," Carl Breer wrote in the auto-biography he completed ten years prior to his death in 1970, "its many innovations were quickly adopted by competition on their own new cars."

That the Airflow was a success in all factors that matter, however, is the credo of the Airflow Club of America. Its six hundred members have spread the gospel and enjoyed the cars since 1962. The Airflow seen here is owned by Bruce Barnet and is one of three '34 Imperial coupes on the long wheelbase chassis known to exist. The other two are basket cases, as was this one before Airflow enthusiast Stan Block decided to restore it for the challenge and the car's historic interest. "A rewarding experience" was how Stan described the result. At the Annual Meet of the Airflow Club in Arkansas in 2005, the Imperial coupe took four trophies, including Best of Show and People's Choice.

Rewarding indeed.

– BRK

Top: To provide promotional fodder, Chrysler signed up racing driver Harry Hartz, who set 72 AAA records at Bonneville in an Airflow.

Bottom: Chrysler's Highland Park wind tunnel was used to test scale models for aerodynamic drag.

1935 AUBURN 851 SPEEDSTER

While cogitating at Walden Pond, Thoreau concluded it was characteristic of wisdom not to do desperate things. Henry D. was not at the Auburn Automobile Company in 1934, however, when desperate measures were clearly called for and resulted in a sleek speedster.

Streamlining, by definition, involves technical science; this Auburn's streamlining was wrought more by alchemy. The exigent circumstances were these. The company had spent a half million dollars in 1933 to redesign the following season's new Auburns, and management hadn't liked the results. Despite a sales increase, the money spent

for the new line cut into profits and made for another huge overall loss.

The Auburn cashbox being largely empty meant that revamping the '34 into a new car had to be done on a *carte* that was anything but *blanche*. Auburn Vice President Harold Ames, the man in charge—as Errett Lobban Cord saw to other enterprises in his far-flung empire—called in Gordon Buehrig, who designed a massive radiator grille and new hood. With these changes, the '35 Auburn line was marched into dealer showrooms in September of '34.

Automobile show time was approaching, however, and Auburn needed a "bomb," in Buehrig's well chosen word, to be noticed among all the other automakers showing off their wares. Speedsters always attracted attention. Upon occasion, Auburn had offered one in its lineup since the late Twenties. Aware of the hundred or so speedster bodies finished in prime and upholstered in muslin, left over from the 1933 version, Harold Ames remembered how much he had liked the boattail speedsters Buehrig had done for Duesenberg. The designer was summoned.

"The body of the Auburn Speedster was inspired by race cars of the period," Gordon wrote to the author several decades ago. "The fenders were designed with the flavor of the coverings of the wheels on the fixed landing gear of small aircraft." Race cars of the period, being of modest hp, demanded wind-cheating bodies that used as little of the engine's energy as possible to push the air out of the way—and air currents were of paramount importance to aircraft. This was aerodynamic science. The rest of the Speedster was sly and crafty.

Buehrig used his Duesenberg Weymann Speedster design as a theme. The impressive grille of the 1935 Auburn was joined to a redesigned hood required because the '33 Speedster body was narrower than the '35. Fenders were formed into a teardrop. Just aft

GORDON
BUEHRIG

of the top well compartment, the '33 body was lopped off, and a new tail designed in clay. Gordon would have liked a new instrument panel but there wasn't the money, nor the time, for that matter.

To meet the schedule, the entire design had to be finished in two weeks, which was accomplished with heavy overtime. More overtime was expended to hand-build four cars for the shows. The public was entranced. Showgoers flocked to the Auburn stand, many of whom also looked at the practical models that they would be more likely to buy. Some of the audience said the car they most wanted to buy was the Speedster. This was really good news. Selling the Speedster would use up the body inventory; the Speedster would be the Auburn "image" car to lure people into showrooms. Dealers, put off by its impracticality, were not enthusiastic and had to be compelled to accept one for their showrooms.

The Speedster was produced in lots of ten or twenty for a total that has been estimated at as few as 150 and as high as 500+. Probably we shall never know the correct figure. "These [cars] were largely handmade," Gordon Buehrig related, "with only very cheap hardware draw forms used on a hydraulic arch press to form the body tail end panels and the fenders."

The beautiful proportions of the car concealed its massive build, and only by sitting in it did many recognize how high the car's center of gravity was. Not that it mattered. "Every line of this super-charged Auburn indicates speed and racyness [sic]," reported *Automobile Topics*, a conclusion certain to attract stereotypical extroverts, movie stars and sports figures in particular. Among the latter was golfer Walter Hagen, who well knew showmanship and

generally managed to arrive at a tournament at the last possible moment, speeding to a stop at the first tee, leaping out of the Speedster, grabbing a club from his caddy, and executing an impressive drive with the Auburn behind him to document he was an all-around sportsman.

No question, the Auburn Speedster was an attractive proposition to those who wanted and could afford to make a statement. The announced price of $2,245 seems to have been optimistically low and much less than most purchasers paid. But, in addition to the racy coachwork, the price included the Switzer-Cummins supercharger Augie Duesenberg and Pearl Watson had adapted for Auburn, and which added handsomely to the power of the car's 279.9-cubic-inch Lycoming straight-eight.

The company advertised, and the press happily reiterated, that every Auburn Speedster had been driven better than 100 mph prior to delivery. As late as 1949, land-speed record ace Ab Jenkins insisted he had been behind the wheel of "each and every one of the cars" and didn't get out until he made the 100+ mark "through the measured mile." A plaque attesting to the speed was affixed to each Speedster built. Although Auburn as an automobile manufacturer had passed into history in 1936, Jenkins was still obviously a company man. Body draftsman Dick Robinson subsequently revealed that on a stroll through the body assembly shop, he saw a workman "energetically tacking plates on the instrument panels, although the bodies still had not been mounted on the chassis."

There's no way to know when the plaque on this Speedster was fitted. Formerly in the S. Ray Miller collection, the car was acquired at auction two years ago by Sam Mann. He doesn't care about the plaque details but is anxious to demonstrate the truth of the mph figure at the first opportunity.
– BRK

Opposite page, bottom: Each Auburn 851 Speedster carried a plaque certifying that it had been driven at 100 mph by record-breaker Ab Jenkins.

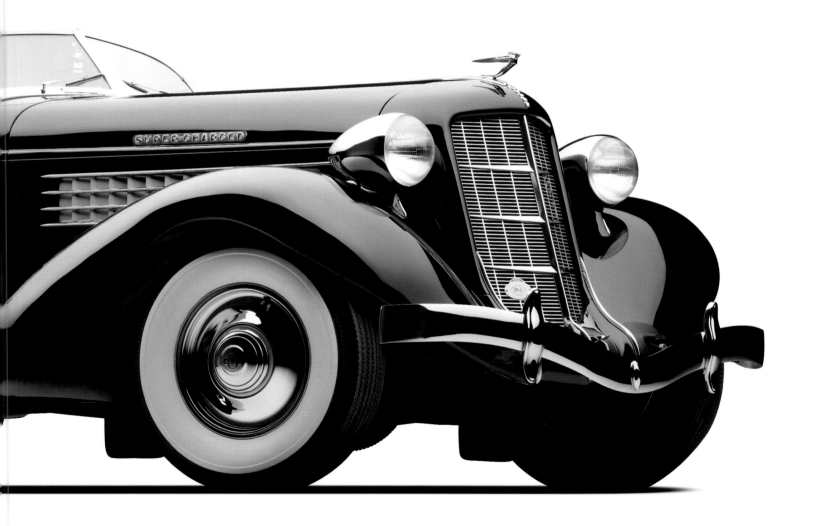

1936 STOUT SCARAB

In 1935, there was nothing else like the Stout Scarab. With the flat-head Ford engine tucked in the tail of the beetle-like contraption, the entire capacious interior remained for accommodating people. From the outside, the Scarab looked more like it was built by an airplane designer than by an automaker.

Technical journalist, automotive engineer and airplane designer, William Stout served as chief engineer of Packard's aircraft division during World War I. Following the war, in 1919, Stout designed a high-winged monoplane without the struts and wires that had characterized earlier aircraft.

The Stout Engineering Company continued its work on the all-metal airplane and, eventually, the Stout Air Sedan. Using Stout-built aircraft, in 1925 Ford launched an air freight service between Detroit and Chicago. Later that year, Ford bought Stout's company. Stout's design for a three-engined commercial aircraft served as the inspiration for the very successful Ford Tri-Motor.

Meanwhile, Stout had also founded Stout Air Services to provide regularly-scheduled passenger service between Detroit and Grand Rapids. Service was later added to Chicago and Cleveland. After selling the airline to United in

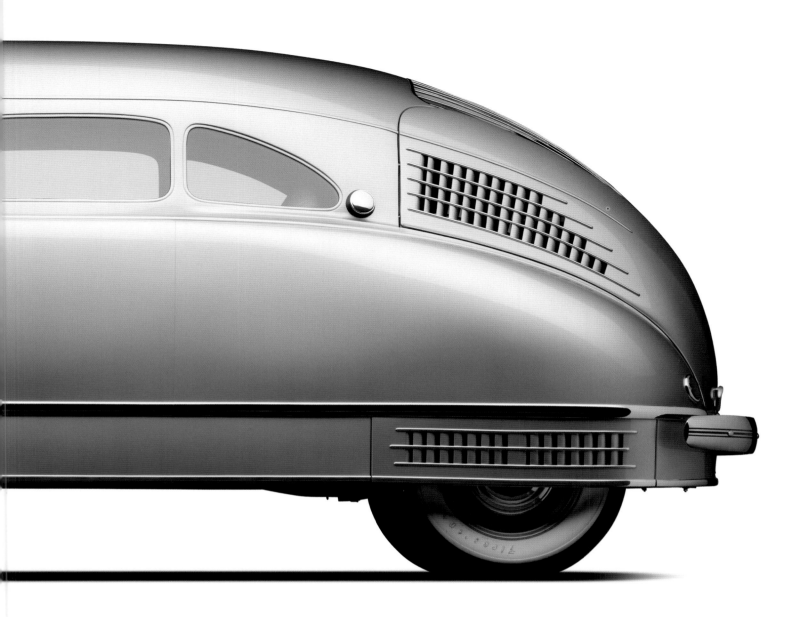

1929, Stout re-established his engineering laboratory in Dearborn. Initially, efforts focused on aviation, but by the early 1930s, Stout had resolved to build what automobile historian Tom LaMarre called "an automobile employing the latest aviation technology."

Inspired by aviation techniques, the Scarab—named after the hard-shelled Egyptian beetle—with its metal panels over a framework of tubing, took much of its strength from what was essentially an exoskeleton. The front suspension used coil springs and was similar to the later MacPherson Strut configuration. Rear suspension relied on a pair of transverse leaf springs. The four-wheel drum brakes were power-assisted.

Power for the Scarab came from Ford's 221 cid, 85 bhp flathead V-8, which transmitted power to Ford's three-speed manual transmission by way of a custom transfer case using a six-row chain. The engine was reversed and the radiator is positioned in the rear of the car. Ford also supplied many other components, including the 16-inch steel wheels that were partially obscured by the skirting of the body's lower edge.

Although the rear-engined layout was indeed revolutionary, the packaging of the interior and the exterior styling were positively astonishing for the time. With its snub nose and cabin shape, the Scarab showed a closer resemblance to Stout's Safety Plane than to any earth-bound vehicle.

The Scarab—which predates the modern mini-van by roughly half a century—could be entered through the driver's door or through one on the passenger side. Only the driver's seat and rear bench were fixed. The other two chairs could be positioned at will in the commodious interior. The view forward and to the sides was excellent, while rear vision was limited at best.

WILLIAM
STOUT

Unlike its rolling contemporaries, the Scarab incorporated its fenders into the main body design and dispensed with running boards. The smooth design dramatically reduced wind resistance and noise, while increasing directional stability. Detailing of the unusual body was superlative, with an intricate scarab motif set into the nose, grilled headlights and elegant rear grillework. The airy interior featured elegant wood trim, a varnished wicker headliner and tubular-framed seats that were usually upholstered in leather.

When new, the exclusive Scarabs (priced upwards of $5,000) were sold by invitation to people of means and influence. With such an exclusive sales arrangement, production was limited—between six and nine cars were built. The original prototype sat for many years and is presumed destroyed, as is Stout's own car. Customer cars went to Stout stockholder and chewing gum king Phillip Wrigley and fellow-investor Willard Dow. Robert Stranahan of Champion Spark Plug also owned one, as did Harvey Firestone. Car number 5 was shipped directly to France for the editor of the *Le Temps* newspaper, while radio host Major Edward Bowes is also believed to have taken delivery of a Scarab.

Having survived the German occupation, the French Scarab was rumored to have been used by Generals de Gaulle and Eisenhower. Although it sported American and French flags, there's no proof that the Scarab ever served in an official capacity. Subsequently, the Scarab is supposed to have housed monkeys for a circus, which is unlikely, considering the excellent condition of the original wood trim and wicker headliner.

By 1951 or 1952, the car was sitting in a used car lot in Paris, where American Robert Straub photographed it. Within a few years, it had passed to the collection of French industrial and automotive designer Phillippe Charbonneaux, where it remained.

In the mid-1990s, Charbonneaux unsuccessfully sent the car to auction. American collector Larry Smith had long wanted the French Scarab and, in 1995, Smith had a chance meeting with Charbonneaux's son at the Goodwood Festival of speed. Despite initial encouragement, Smith was still unsuccessful in repatriating the Scarab until collector car connoisseur Christian Philippsen set up a dinner with the Charbonneaux family in late 1996. A deal was quickly sealed.

When Smith went to customs to pick up the car, he was heavily armed with documentation to convince a dubious customs inspector that the odd beetle-shaped vehicle had been built in the United States. Instead, the car was cleared after the inspector asked "Why would you want this piece of junk?"

With attention to the brakes, ignition and carburetion, the car was soon running. After sitting for a year, the flathead V-8, transmission and chain-drive transfer case were overhauled by Michigan restorer Brian Josephs of Classic & Exotic Service, Inc. Meanwhile, the body was tackled by Smith's own Autometric Collision. Once the body was completed, Classic & Exotic completed the assembly and retrimmed the interior. Following the car's completion in May 2003, it has been shown at Amelia Island, Bagatelle in France, Meadow Brook Hall and the Glenmoor Gathering, where it is a consistent crowd favorite. With a shape that is still startling in the 21st century, for many years it was incredibly popular as a tin toy available from several manufacturers.

– JAS

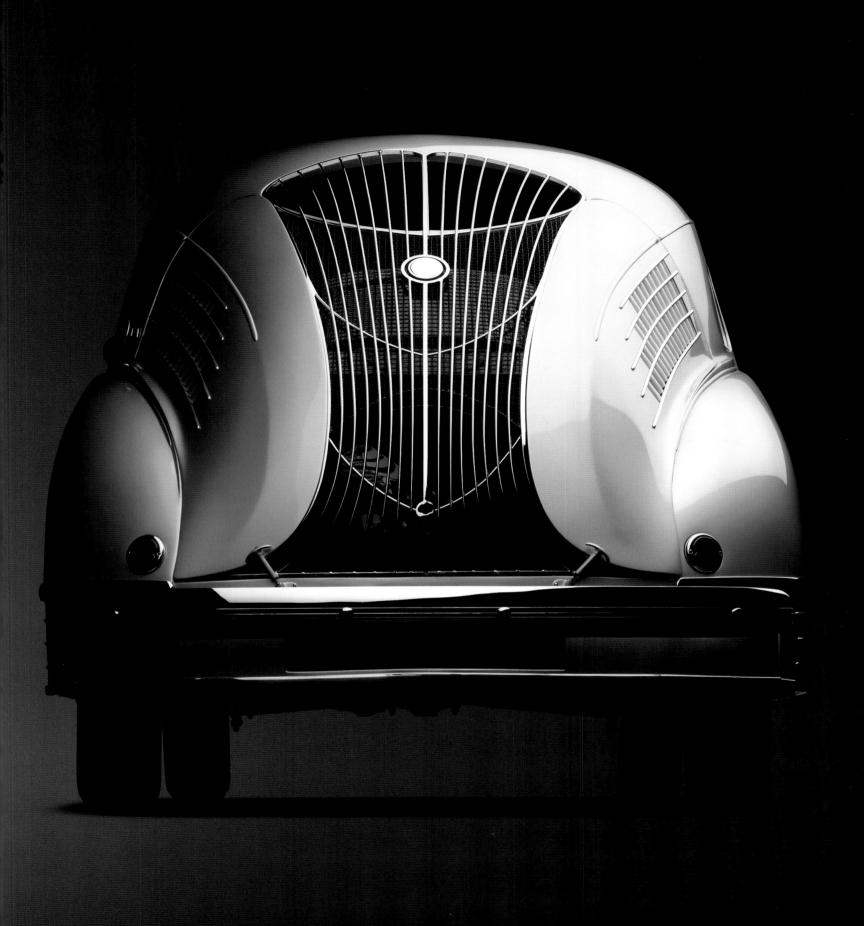

1937 CORD 812 ROADSTER

In 1936 *The Autocar*, the British motoring journal not known for overstatement, called the new Cord "the most unorthodox car in the world today." Seven decades later it can be argued that, among those with even a modicum of awareness about automobiles of the past, the car remains the most recognizable one on the planet.

"A tricky body" was what Harold Ames had asked for in September 1933. Then president of Duesenberg, Inc., Ames envisioned a smaller, less pricey version of the Model J using a modified Auburn chassis. Adding revenue to the company coffers now that the Great Depression was firmly

settled unto the land was urgently needed. The project was enticing enough for erstwhile Duesenberg designer Gordon Buehrig to be persuaded back from General Motors where he had earlier defected. How the rear drive "baby" Duesenberg metamorphosed into the front drive Cord is an interesting tale.

When Ames said "tricky" to Buehrig, Gordon showed him the GM Art & Colour design contest entry of a car with a sealed engine compartment and radiator mounted in the area between hood and fenders. The contest judges had hated it, GM designers loved it—and so did Ames. Buehrig

was given the green light to proceed, as Ames contacted Lycoming for the baby Duesenberg's engine and took chief engineer Bill Baster's suggestion for a 90-degree V-8 cast in a single block. It was now November.

The order to build Buehrig's design was placed with body builder A.H. Walker on January 19, 1934. Two weeks later, an Auburn eight-cylinder chassis arrived at the Duesenberg plant in Indianapolis, and Augie Duesenberg began putting a car together. Meanwhile, Errett Lobban Cord had given Ames the executive vice presidency of the Auburn Automobile Company. He was now in charge of seeing to the financial health of both Duesenberg and Auburn.

In Auburn, Indiana, Ames became aware of Project E-278, a front drive Auburn using concepts Cornelius Van Ranst had developed for the Cord L-29 of 1929-30. Ames recognized the Buehrig baby Duesenberg body as the ideal complement to the Auburn front-drive chassis. He didn't hesitate. Although an Auburn man for a comparative nano-second, Ames stole the Buehrig body from the company of his first allegiance.

Lycoming was apprised of the switch to front drive and made changes accordingly. Buehrig, who had been taken in tow to Auburn by Ames to redesign its '34 model line for '35 (which included the 851 Speedster shown elsewhere in this book), was now head of Auburn's design department. His new assignment was creating a body for the front-drive Auburn based on, but not simply revised from, the baby Duesenberg.

"Styling is sculpture to me," Buehrig once said. As an "artist," he was given an ideal canvas upon which to work. The light suspension loads at the rear of a front drive car lent itself admirably to unit-body construction, a layout that was lighter in weight, with increased overall stiffness and better crash protection for passengers. For the body designer, the configuration meant no driveshaft for a lower stance as well as an entry into the automobile that Hudson would ballyhoo as "step down" a decade-and-a-half later.

The remarkable aspects of the new car's body have been limned so often through the years as to produce ennui, so here a simple recitation will suffice: concealed headlamps, disappearing convertible top, flush taillights and gas hatch, absence of running boards, concealed door hinges, pontoon fenders and sloping rear deck. More interesting was how effortlessly these elements seemed to combine into a homogenous streamlined whole. The Cord was not tested in a wind tunnel. Indeed, aerodynamics was not a word Gordon Buehrig used in talking about the car. "A natural solution," he said. "A functional design." The Cord was as radical as Mies van der Rohe's Barcelona chair and Frank Lloyd Wright's building for Johnson Wax in Racine, Wisconsin. And, like those icons of the modern age, the Cord made sublime good sense.

The final design of the new car received management approval late in 1934. The company board nixed further development the following January. The only member of the board who really mattered, however, was E.L. Cord. He had been enamored of front drive since the L-29; since that car had carried his name, so should this one—and it would go into manufacture.

Precious time had passed, and the rush to get cars ready for the show circuit took on an aura of the stampede to the Klondike. Once the shows proved the Cord a sensation, the rush into production was no less frantic. It is no exaggeration to suggest the new car's test drivers were its first customers. The car had more than a few "issues" (as "problems" are called today), and fewer people were at Auburn to deal with them. No one there could fail to be aware of the company's financial straits. Recognizing their jobs might soon be in peril, senior members of Auburn's engineering department left. So did Gordon Buehrig.

The 1936 Cord had been designated the 810. The 1937 car was called the 812 and could be had with a supercharger (a modified Switzer-Cummins unit, like the Auburn 851 Speedster). All was for naught. By year's end, the Cord joined the recently departed Auburn and the Duesenberg as artifacts of history. But not before Ab Jenkins drove a stock supercharged Cord a full day and a full night over the bricks at Indianapolis for a new speed record of 79.577 mph, which won the company the coveted Stevens Trophy. Not only was the Cord a dazzling design, it was dazzlingly fast.

There are those who believe every serious automobile collection should have a Cord 810/812. Ray Scherr thinks so. This supercharged 812 dazzled him, and he added it to his estimable California collection several years ago.

—BRK

Following spread: The Cord 810 and later 812 (shown) were developed from the original Gordon Buehrig drawings for the car that was to be the "baby" Duesenberg.

Oct. 2, 1934.

Fig.1

Des. 93,451

G. M. BUEHRIG
AUTOMOBILE
Filed May 17, 1934

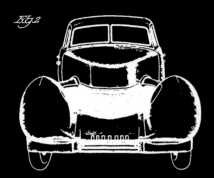
Fig.2

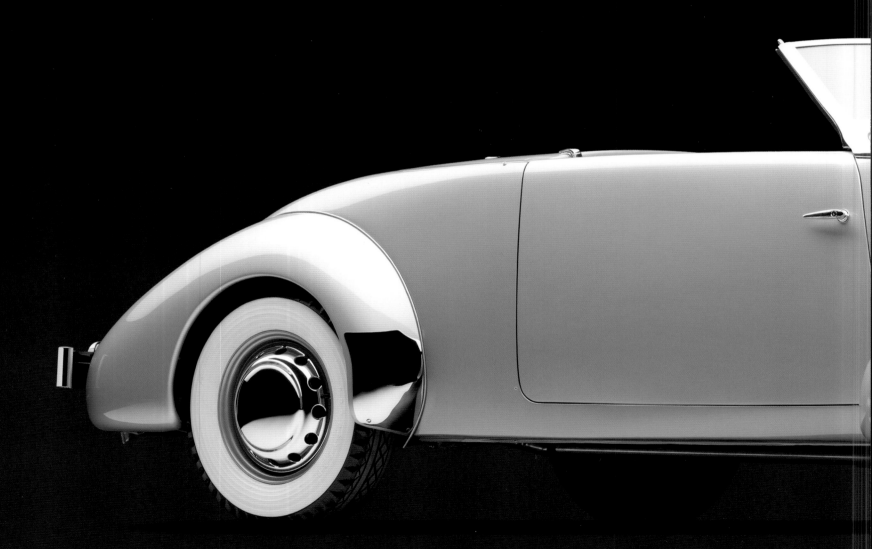

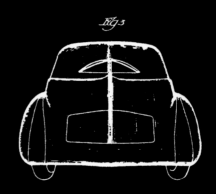

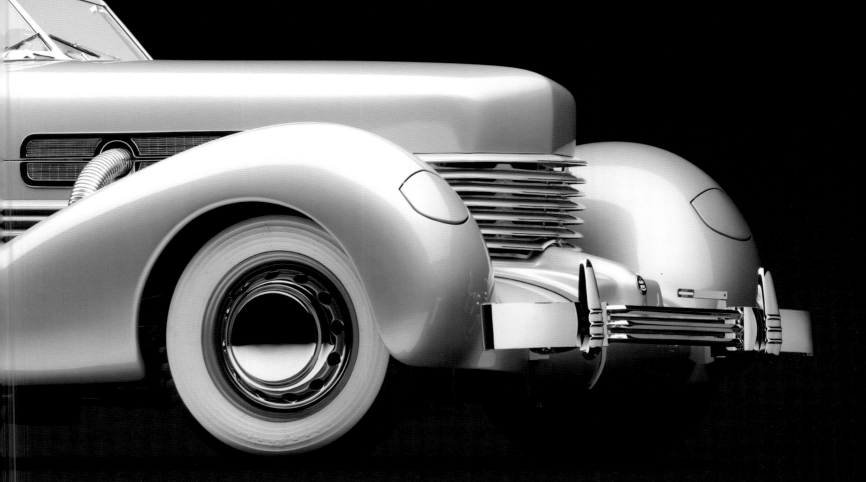

1939 LINCOLN ZEPHYR COUPE

The Lincoln Zephyr was an enormously important car to Ford Motor Company. It gave the Dearborn automaker a third model line that was fully competitive with contemporary General Motors and Chrysler offerings. The original Lincoln Zephyr of 1936 also proved that the science of aerodynamics, tempered by the art of streamline design, *could* sell in the showroom. A new and trend-setting frontal appearance would grace the 1938 Zephyr. The 1939-1941 models that followed would be some of the most beautiful streamlined automobiles ever.

The 1933 aerodynamic study that was the genesis for the Zephyr didn't start out as a Lincoln, had

not been a Ford Motor Company project, and certainly could not be considered beautiful. But that was all before Edsel Ford came into the picture.

The origins of the Lincoln Zephyr trace back to the early work of John Tjaarda, a legendary designer of teardrop shaped, aerodynamically-sound automobiles. The first of his "Sterkenberg" designs—named after a family estate in Holland—had appeared in 1926.

By the early 1930s, Tjaarda was employed by Briggs Manufacturing, which designed and built bodies for Detroit automakers. His mission was to

create studies that challenged conventional automotive design, both in appearance and in construction. In 1933, he revealed his most advanced Sterkenberg ever, which was shown as the Briggs Dream Car. This aerodynamic, rear-engined fastback sedan showcased innovative aircraft-inspired unit-body construction that eliminated a separate chassis frame.

Briggs showed the new Sterkenberg to Edsel Ford—son of Henry, president of Ford Motor Company and patron/protector of Ford and Lincoln designers. Edsel happened to be looking for a new car that could offset the sales collapse the terrible economy of the early 1930s had inflicted on the luxurious Lincoln. He realized the Sterkenberg could become the car Ford needed.

Rights to produce the design were quickly arranged.

The Sterkenberg's smoothly tapered sedan body could be essentially produced as designed. However, Edsel was adamant that its stubby "sheep's nose" front end be restyled. When Tjaarda proved intractable, Ford designer E.T. "Bob" Gregorie was drafted to help translate the Sterkenberg into a front-engined production vehicle. Gregorie, only 24 at the time, was already well on his way to becoming the leader of Ford's nascent design department. He was well attuned to Edsel's design preferences and quickly sketched a new frontal appearance—an "ironing board" hood extending out over a tall and sharply V'eed grille. The new prow-like ensemble would completely change the look of the car. It was simple... simple genius.

The new car also needed a new name. Inspiration was found in the Burlington Zephyr passenger train, which had helped popularize *Streamline Moderne* design with its successful showing at the 1934 Chicago World's Fair. Ford borrowed the name for the new car and called it the Lincoln Zephyr.

By the time the new Lincoln Zephyr was launched in late 1935, the Great Depression was easing. America was a nation moving forward again. Travel—by air, rail or highway—was fashionable. Streamline design both encouraged and reflected this spirit of motion. Even the newest household appliances looked as if they were, "doing 60 standing still."

JOHN
TJAARDA

The Zephyr was significant in more than appearance. It was the first unit-body car produced in North America. An exceptionally low floor allowed most passengers to step directly into the vehicle and the narrow running boards were hardly needed.

Another "first" was scored with the Zephyr's single-piece, rear-hinged "alligator" hood. Opening it revealed a 268 cid L-head V-12 engine, a close relative of the Ford "flathead" V8. The Zephyr chassis also shared significant engineering features with the Ford.

The new Zephyr was available initially only in two- and four-door sedan models. The roomy sedan was priced at $1,320—less than half the price of any previous or contemporary traditional Lincoln. A handsome three-passenger coupe joined the line in 1937, followed the next year by a convertible coupe and convertible sedan.

In 1938, the Lincoln Zephyr again caught the rest of the American auto industry by surprise. The new model sported a split grille, mounted low in a horizontal opening. The look was much envied. Over at GM, Harley Earl was reportedly furious that a competitor had scored such a major styling coup. Within two years, variations would appear on most American cars. Many decades later, designer Gregorie would tell biographer Henry Dominguez how the grille that changed the face of American automobiles

came to be: the V-12 engine's low-mounted cooling fan needed better airflow.

Further refinement for 1939 produced an especially compelling Zephyr. A revised grille featured thin vertical bars. To enhance visual unity, the essentially vestigial running boards were now concealed with metal extensions.

When Edsel Ford wanted a unique vehicle for use at his family's Florida property, he asked Bob Gregorie to start with a 1939 Zephyr. The resulting car proved so wildy popular, that it became the prototype for the car that entered production in 1940 as the Lincoln Continental. The beautiful Continental was continued for 1941 and 1942 and resumed production from 1946-1948 and is considered highly collectible today.

The 1942 Zephyr models, the last before WWII, would move away from streamlining, with less rounded fenders and a new, bolder front end. After the war, the 1946-1948 Lincoln would continue the 1942 appearance, enhanced with a new grille design. Post-war editions would not use the Zephyr name.

To many, the 1939 Type 72 coupe is the loveliest of all the Zephyrs. Present owner Ray Scherr recalls being taken with the burgundy coupe's "swooping" roofline and long, curvaceous deck when he encountered it at a Michigan auction. "It stopped me in my tracks," he says. The coupe was soon on its way to Westlake Village, California, where it would join the Scherr collection of exceptional classic cars.

By 1951, the Museum of Modern Art in New York would be hailing the Lincoln Zephyr as "The first successful streamline car in America." More than 180,000 Lincolns based on the 1933 Sterkenberg had been built, each one a tribute to the men who had brought science and art together in the original 1936 Lincoln Zephyr.

— TVB

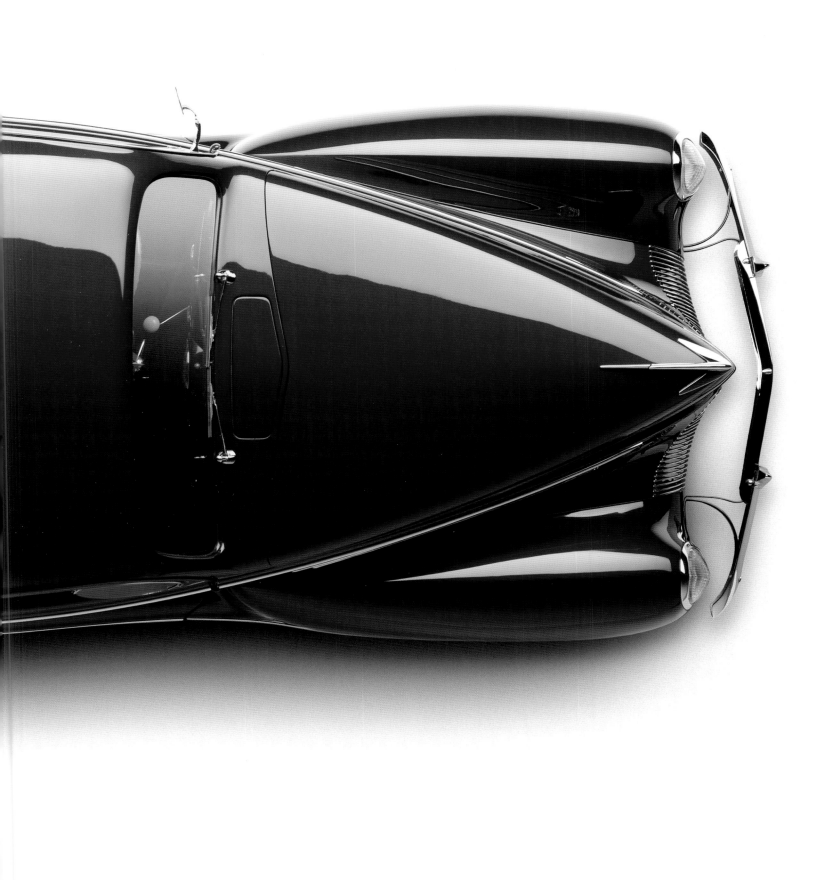

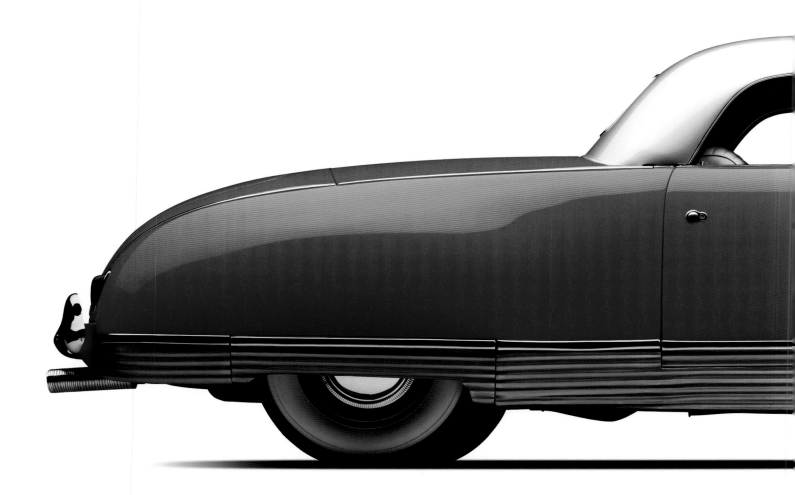

1941 CHRYSLER THUNDERBOLT

In October 1940, Chrysler created a sensation by revealing not one, but two, stunning show cars at the New York National Auto Show. Named the Thunderbolt and the Newport, they were beautiful expressions of streamline design at its zenith. Yet, they were quite different in appearance. The Thunderbolt and Newport were among the earliest examples of what we now call concept cars. Chrysler had several of each built to maintain an aggressive schedule of auto show and dealer exhibits that often drew crowds numbering in the thousands. Remarkably, once the tours were finished, these special show cars would be sold to private owners.

Chrysler called the Thunderbolt convertible roadster "The Car of The Future." It was not an exaggeration—there had never been a car like it. Its smoothly aerodynamic "envelope" body, concealed headlamps and retractable one-piece metal hardtop were only some of its innovations. The Newport 4-door phaeton, with its voluptuous curves, notched doors and twin flat windshields that folded down, was inspired by the sporty dual-cowl phaetons of the early '30s—it was "retro" design, 1940 style!

The cars were constructed for Chrysler by LeBaron, a highly regarded coachbuilding concern

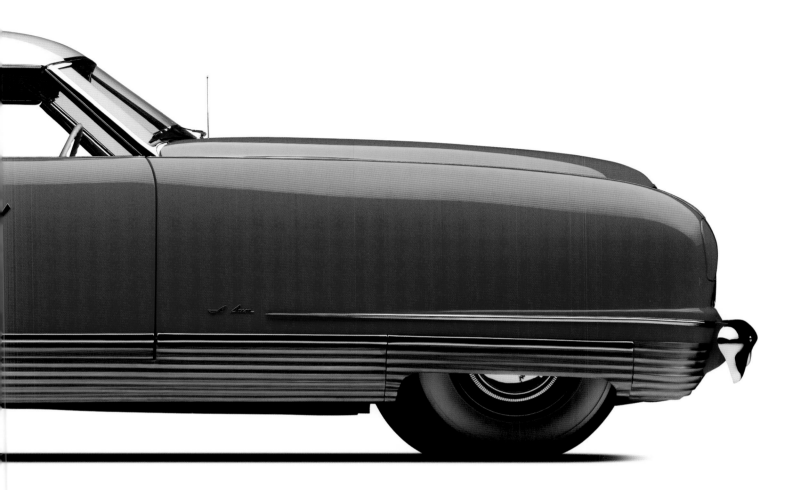

operated as a Briggs Manufacturing affiliate. Based in Detroit, Briggs made production bodies for Chrysler, Packard and Ford, among others. They also offered their clients advanced design services.

A Chrysler introductory brochure for the Thunderbolt and Newport credited the cars to LeBaron's then chief designer Ralph Roberts, who had been drafting and building custom bodies for twenty years. Respected for his extraordinary ability to finesse designs, Roberts had helped shape many cars now regarded as classics. There was more to the story, though. We know now that Roberts had partnered with a young designer named Alex Tremulis to create the cars. Tremulis, who at the time worked for Briggs,

would eventually be recognized as one of the most visionary stylists of his time.

Roberts and Tremulis began sketching the cars that would become the Thunderbolt and Newport during 1939. During a presentation of their ideas to Chrysler Corporation President K. T. Keller and division head David Wallace, Tremulis proposed that the dramatically streamlined cars be positioned as "new milestones in Airflow design." Within this context, the often-criticized 1934 Airflow could be justly portrayed as an important step in the evolution of streamline design. The Chrysler executives enthusiastically approved the program, but threw in a caveat: both cars would have to be ready for the New York

RALPH ROBERTS

show, which was only months away.

One admirer has called the Thunderbolt "beyond futuristic." Indeed, with its extremely clean lines, somewhat robot-like frontal appearance and lighting-bolt door appliqués, the Thunderbolt seemed like the sort of car a fictional super hero would drive. (During World War II, co-designer Alex Tremulis would create "flying saucer" concepts for the military. And, after the war, he would become chief designer for another car of the future—the ill-fated Tucker '48).

The Thunderbolt's electrically retractable steel top was a first for an American car. At the touch of a button, the mechanism, patented by Roberts, lifted a metal panel and rotated the top down into a storage compartment. The silver-painted top complemented the fluted lower body trim, which virtually encircled the car with a broad band of anodized satin silver.

A one-piece curved windshield, mounted into an elegantly simple frame, was years ahead of its time. Side windows were raised hydraulically. There were no vent windows or wind deflectors. Doors were opened via pushbuttons, inside and out.

The hood stretched from windshield base to front bumper in a single panel and was also exceptionally wide. To eliminate a traditional grille, the air intakes were located below the bumper.

Shrouded front wheels were another prominent Thunderbolt feature. However, to ensure that the front wheels could turn fully, they were inset. Although wind tunnel testing proved that skirted wheels reduced drag, this futuristic touch would never really catch on.

Inside, the Thunderbolt had a well-appointed interior with single bench seat for three. A full set of Lucite-faced, backlit gauges was spread across the dash.

With the New York show looming, LeBaron constructed the Thunderbolt (and Newport) using traditional coachbuilding methods—metal panels were applied over a wooden framework.

Above: Ralph Roberts was responsible for the design of Chrysler's futuristic Thunderbolt. One of the Thunderbolt's most distinctive elements was the all-steel retractable roof, which was unheard of in 1941.

The hood and deck lid were steel, with the rest of the body formed in aluminum. Thanks to what was no doubt a marathon effort by all concerned, the first cars were finished in time for the New York show, which opened on October 6, 1940.

Powering the Thunderbolt was a 323.5 cid Chrysler Imperial L-head Spitfire straight-eight, rated at 140 hp. An early production Fluid Drive transmission offered semi-automatic shifting plus an overdrive range.

Chrysler originally announced that eight Thunderbolts would be built. However, only five were completed, along with six Newport phaetons. Following their very successful promotional tours, all were released for sale to private owners. The Thunderbolt's list price was quoted at $8,250 in an October 1940 press release.

The exhibit Thunderbolt is owned by Judge Joseph C. Cassini, III and his wife, Margie, of New Jersey.

The fourth Thunderbolt built, its provenance from new is well established. A Chrysler dealer in Chicago obtained it from the factory and sold it to the vice president of Mexico in 1942. Sometime in the mid-1960s, it returned to the U.S. and passed into collector hands. Around 1980, the car was for a time owned by the son of the original selling dealer. Ownership by several prominent collectors followed and, by 2005, the Thunderbolt had been meticulously restored and had won several prestigious show awards. It remains the only one of the four surviving examples to be finished in an original color scheme.

When Judge Cassini discovered that Thunderbolt number 4 was to be offered at auction in early 2006, he recognized an exceedingly rare opportunity to add one of the earliest and most significant concept cars ever to his exceptional collection of European and American classics.

– TVB

TUCKER '48

Long before there was even a factory, the Tucker Torpedo was first constructed almost entirely in the mind of Preston Thomas Tucker. It was to be ultra modern in design, with three headlamps that followed the direction in which the car was turned. Suspension was to be fully-independent; brakes would be discs and a potent rear-mounted, fuel-injected six-cylinder engine would power the car via hydraulic drive. What's more, the car was to be capable of very high speeds and provide its occupants with levels of safety unprecedented in the 1940s.

Although the source of inspiration for the car, later known as the Tucker '48, was clearly with

entrepreneur and super-salesman Preston Tucker, he was not a trained engineer. The Michigan farm boy left school at an early age and had many different careers—office boy for Cadillac, police officer, autoworker and mechanic—before he found his true calling. By all accounts, Tucker was charming, engaging and a natural salesman. Once on the selling side of the new car business, his success began. From there, he joined forces with Harry Miller to build the front-wheel drive Miller-Ford racing cars. With war approaching, he also conceived and built a prototype of a high-speed troop-carrying combat car. Although it was rejected by the military for being too fast, its gun turret design was accepted and Tucker

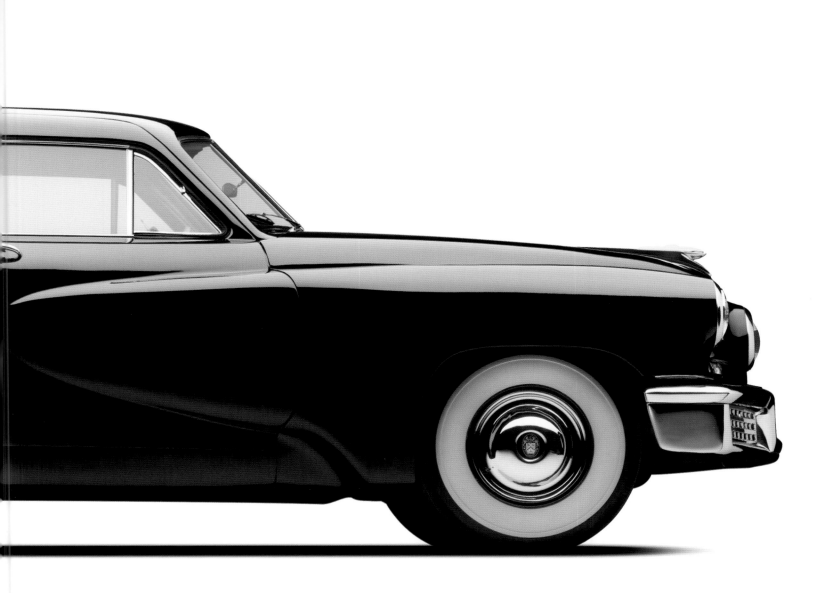

soon found himself in the manufacturing business.

After the war, Tucker, who had always been enamored by the automobile, dreamed of a car that would be modern and exciting and coincide with the pent-up demand caused by four wartime years without new vehicles. But, because he was a salesman and not a stylist or engineer, the task of translating his vision into reality fell to a team of people. The men responsible for the original Tucker engine and the chassis design are largely unknown, although an array of designers contributed to the shape that eventually became the Tucker '48.

The first man other than Preston Tucker to influence the design of the Tucker car was George Lawson, a graduate of the Cleveland Institute of Art and an alumnus of Buick design. As Director of Styling for Tucker, he was responsible for the first renderings and models based on Preston Tucker's input. His initial work showed a shape with a pointed prow tipped by a center headlamp. That nose quickly widened as it reached back to accommodate a passenger compartment evoking the cockpit of a fighter plane. The entire shape was very much like a separate fuselage, with fender nacelles that stood proud of the body. Although they were not feasible for production, originally those front fenders were intended to turn with the wheels.

Lawson left Tucker in December 1946 and was soon replaced by Auburn-Cord-Duesenberg alumnus Alex Tremulis. Rather than starting from scratch, his work was very much evolutionary and

ALEX TREMULIS

was supplemented by the New York design consultancy of J. Gordon Lippincott and Company, which sent a crew to Chicago that included Read Viemeister, Hal Bergstrom, Tucker P. Madawick, Budd Steinhilber and Philip S. Egan.

In an odd dynamic, Tremulis and the Lippincott team shared ideas while developing competing concepts and full-size clay models. Ultimately, the design chosen was a combination of the concepts of the Tremulis and Lippincott proposals, which in turn had been heavily influenced by the work of George Lawson. Undoubtedly, though, both Lawson and Tucker must have seen the Tatra T77, which used a center headlamp, and shared the basic chassis layout of a large rear-mounted engine and fully-independent suspension.

While the design work progressed, the mechanical development lagged behind as the Tucker-designed engine proved underpowered and generally unsatisfactory. At the eleventh hour, a helicopter engine from Aircooled Motors of Syracuse, New York, was adapted to water-cooling and substituted for the in-house engine. Additionally, the proposed fuel-injection, electronic ignition and disc brakes were deemed insufficiently developed for use on a passenger car, while the hydraulic drive simply wasn't realistic. Instead, the fuel-air mixture was fed by a carburetor, a conventional mechanical distributor was used and proven hydraulic drum brakes were substituted for the discs. When it came to transmitting power to the rear wheels, a modified Cord transaxle was used, while a Tucker engineer worked feverishly to develop a full automatic gearbox to work with the rear-engine configuration.

All the efforts of Tucker and his upstart company came to nothing when, on June 6, 1948, a Security and Exchange Commission investigation resulted in the shutdown of the Tucker Corporation. By that time, 37 pilot Tucker '48 cars had been built, although an additional 14 were later completed from parts on hand. Tucker, and the executives who were his co-defendants, were ultimately acquitted of all charges. However, by the time the case was closed in 1950, Tucker had lost his factory, his funding and his dream.

Although the original design brief for the Tucker '48 had been to create a modern, exciting and safe new automobile, aerodynamics had not been a major concern. Once the design was completed and being readied for production, a scale model was wind-tunnel tested to observe airflow and determine the ideal placement for the radiator. According to former Lippincott and Tucker Corporation designer Philip Egan, the wind-tunnel exercise found that "the drag coefficient, the measure of the Tucker '48's streamlining, was remarkably advanced for its time."

Of the 51 Tucker '48s completed, car number 1030 is a part of the Petersen Automotive Museum's collection. It is said to have been Preston Tucker's personal car, which is quite likely considering that he also retained car number 1029. Fortunately, 1030 is frequently displayed as a complete and running example of what could have been the car of the future.

– JAS

The Tucker '48 . . . The Car You Have Been Waiting For

You've waited long years for a really new car. *Here it is* . . . completely new, yet with engineering principles completely proved in 15 years of rigid tests.

Yes, and you've waited for a car that would give you as much for your money as before the war. The Tucker '48 does that *and more.* It's finer, more luxurious than the most expensive cars of today, yet priced in the medium field. It has a 128" wheelbase, is 5' high from road to roof, and delivers 30 to 35 miles per gallon at moderate driving speed.

Later this very year, this exciting new car will be ready to drive . . . ready to give you the motoring thrill of your life. Be among the first to give it a workout. You owe it to yourself to get acquainted with a car so completely new in line and design . . . so completely proved in engineering principles . . . that it will still be a leader many years and thousands upon thousands of miles from now.

EUROPEAN STREAMLINED CARS

THE EUROPEAN VIEW

The study of aerodynamics began with airplanes and airships and was later applied to trains and automobiles, often by the same men who had shaped aircraft. Although increasingly aerodynamic shapes ventured onto race tracks early in the 20th century, streamlined automobiles for the road really began to evolve during the late 1920s and into the 1930s.

A public that had suf-fered through economic, political and armed upheaval hungered for something new, and streamlined styling was exciting and modern. Automobiles were transformed from utilitarian square boxes into brilliantly colored and curvaceous examples of velocity and motion.

A galvanizing event took place in 1925, when the Exposition des Arts Décoratifs in Paris introduced what was known as Art Moderne. For the first time, industrial designers and stylists came together at the cultural center of Europe to display their designs and share ideas. From it evolved a whole new technical vocabulary to describe the new science of aerodynamics and its effects on everyday artifacts. Streamlining became synonymous with speed and power, which, in turn, was linked in the public's mind with progress and personal freedom of movement.

Aerodynamic concepts were tested simultaneously in several countries. Some of the first tests were conducted in wind tunnels in France by Gustave Eiffel, in connection with the early development of airplanes during World War I. In Britain, one of the first wind tunnels was built in 1871 by Frank H. Wenham to experiment with

aircraft wing shapes for gliders. As early as 1899, Étienne-Jules Marey of France used a smoke stream in a tunnel to test the shape of trains. An adaptation of this same technique is still used in automotive wind tunnel experiments to observe airflow around vehicles.

After Germany's defeat in World War I, the terms of the Armistice forbade it from producing  aircraft. Instead, its companies, engineers and technicians were free to focus on automobile development and production. Edmund Rumpler, one of Germany's aerodynamic pioneers, tested automobiles at Gustave Eiffel's research facility, which is where he also tested airships before the Zeppelin Company built its own wind tunnel in 1920.

Hungarian-born Paul Jaray had worked with Rumpler at Zeppelin. After his departure in 1923, he perfomed extensive experimentation and wind-tunnel testing of automotive shapes, which he patented. His first completed streamline design was built on a German Ley chassis. Not only was the car more efficient due to lower wind resistance, it was also a closed coupé at a time when most cars were open. Jaray moved to Switzerland and established the "Stream-Line Carriage Body Company." It was followed by the "Jaray Streamline Corporation" in the United States, where he filed his first patents in 1927. On May 24, 1935, the Jaray Streamline Corporation sued Chrysler for patent infringement connected with the design of the Airflow. Two months later, Chrysler purchased the license for the Airflow that Jaray's designs had influenced.

As the 1930s progressed, streamlined styling was universally accepted, and became connected in the public's mind with everything modern. Norman Bel Geddes, a visionary in the field of American streamlined forms, said, "Speed is the cry of our era, and greater speed one of the goals of tomorrow." The desire for movement, speed and performance fueled a worldwide phenomenon — the widespread construction of paved roads, which, in turn, created a desire for faster cars. With better roads, chassis could be built with less ground clearance and more supple suspensions. These developments also encouraged more refined and increasingly powerful engines. Meanwhile, the experiments of pioneers such as Rumpler and Jaray proved that cars with coachwork with smooth rounded edges performed substantially better and were more fuel efficient.

PAUL
JARAY

France finally pulled ahead of the pack and became recognized around the world as the leader in streamlined coachbuilding. One of the pioneers of the French movement was Jean Andreau, the director of the Aerodynamic Research Center at Chausson. He focused on the theoretical, using his background in mechanical engineering. Although he gave life to an entire movement, he was not widely recognized for his designs during his lifetime. Like Jaray, he developed many prototypes with fastback styling integrated into clean, continuously curving surfaces. His designs were not intended for production but were styling ideas for the future. Andreau's work on the Peugeot 402 is an aerodynamic triumph, and when tested against a standard Peugeot 402, it is found to use 30 percent less fuel. He also was famous for the shape of George Eyston's land-speed record-setting car of 1937 and 1938. Andreau's last prewar project was the Delage V-12 racecar, with coachwork by Labourdette.

Another eminent practitioner of French streamlined styling was Joseph Figoni, who relied more on art and intuition than strict engineering principles. He absorbed the key elements of mundane industrial designs and transformed them into modern and highly marketable creations. The public loved the swooping lines of the astonishing tea pink and pearly white Delahaye Figoni created for the 1936 Paris Auto Salon. Throughout his life he continued to refine his ideas, and perhaps his most perfect design is the Talbot-Lago T150-C-SS Teardrop coupé.

Coachbuilder Marcel Pourtout and his principal stylist, Georges Paulin, used a different technique. Paulin produced full-sized drawings of his automobiles, the so-called *Grand Plans*, which were later translated into full-sized wooden models that he tested at the Meudon and Vickers wind tunnels. Paulin took a more technical approach to the aerodynamic features of his cars and his calculations were very precise. He was a leader in creating streamlined cars that were mass produced by Peugeot as well as custom built by Pourtout. Unlike coachbuilders Figoni and Saoutchik, Paulin avoided chrome ornamentation and kept the design of his cars simple. Flushed in headlights, door handles and trafficators focused attention on the purity of the car's lines.

Across the English Channel, Paulin was held in high esteem by the Bentley Company, which provided the chassis for perhaps his best known creation, the Embiricos Bentley. According to Bob Lutz of General Motors, this Bentley "looks like the modern prototype of a car of today." Built on the company's 4 1/4 Litre chassis, in a startling departure from tradition and, for the first time, the classic Bentley grille was allowed to lean back and flow into the coachwork.

Although late-comers to the streamlined movement, the Italians focused on aesthetics over function. Coachbuilder and designer Pinin Farina created the Alfa Romeo Type 6C-2300 Pescara in 1935, which has a look suggestive of the later

Embiricos Bentley. The car also bears a resemblance to Figoni's teardrop coupés on the Talbot-Lago T150 chassis. The Alfa Romeo 8C-2900-B Berlinetta clothed by Carrozzeria Touring is another fine example of Italian streamlined design, as was its open spider sibling. Both the Talbot-Lago and the 2.9 Alfa were luxury sports cars at the leading edge of the design world.

Many companies had experimented with streamlined shapes, but the Tatra Type 77 of 1934 was the first production car that truly adhered to aerodynamic principles. The Czech company had worked closely with Paul Jaray and was licensed to apply his theories. Unique in the marketplace, the four-door sedan was built on a rear-engine platform and featured a sloping roof line that ran from roof top to tail, including a fin along the spine. Additional aerodynamic features included strategically placed louvers for engine cooling and covered rear wheels. Despite modest power, its maximum speed was 155 kilometers per hour (96.3 mph). The Type 77 evolved into the faster and more refined Type 87 introduced in 1936.

The wind tunnel testing that started a century ago on a very few experimental or advanced vehicles is now incorporated into every vehicle capable of motion. Many of the earliest practitioners of streamlined design, however, relied far more on their eyes than on the nascent science of aerodynamics. To many connoisseurs, however, those shapes—created by the great European coachbuilders between 1930 and 1940—remain the pinnacle of automotive style, elegance and art.

– RA & DM

1936 PEUGEOT 402 DARL'MAT COUPÉ

Emile Darl'mat's passion for automobiles started very early in life. In 1911, when he was 19 years old, he traveled to Paris and started work for Renault. A decade later, he became a Peugeot dealer and set up a small garage where he could indulge his love of tinkering and enhancing the performance of his cars in true hot-rodder style. In 1927 he met coachbuilder Marcel Pourtout, who had established his shop in Bougival, a suburb of Paris that was home to many coachbuilders and mechanics.

Soon afterwards, Emile Darl'mat commissioned a Pourtout-bodied Peugeot, which was shown at his stand at the Paris Auto Salon in 1927. Then, in 1933, he met the designer Georges Paulin who was working with Peugeot and Pourtout at the time. Together these men would go on to produce automotive gems. Their creative friendship was supported by the continued technical and material support Darl'mat received from Peugeot and its factory in Sochaux.

It wasn't long before Darl'mat and Paulin collaborated to produce a new streamlined body using the chassis of the Peugeot 301, which had been introduced in 1932. Virtually simultaneously, Chrysler was working on the design of its ground-

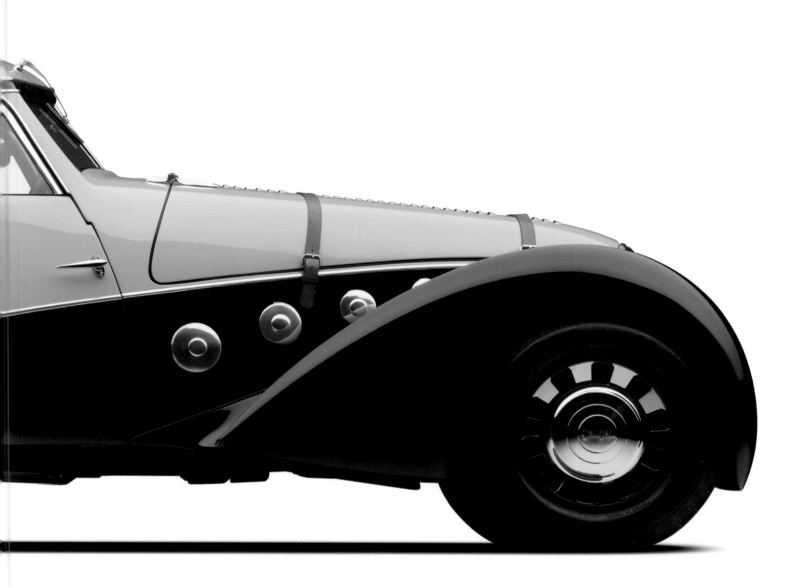

breaking "Chrysler Airflow" model, which would be presented at the 1933-34 Chicago World Fair to great acclaim. Darl'mat and Paulin took note of the aerodynamic design of the Airflow, and its influence is evident in their own final production.

Despite labor problems and strikes in France, November 1936 marked the birth of the team's next great achievement, the 302 Spécial Sport. Georges Paulin was in charge of the body design and Pourtout produced the coachwork in his new shop. Although the 2.2 litre engine in the 302 had been tuned by Darl'mat, it was by no means a competition engine. To compensate for the performance limitations of the engine, Darl'mat challenged Paulin to create a shape that would maximize the car's performance through attention

to aerodynamics. In response, Paulin created a wooden model—which still exists today—which was tested at the wind tunnel in Meudon with great results.

It was about this time that Darl'mat decided on his strategy to offer his clients a car with "the performance of a race car and the price of a regular touring car." In January 1937, the decision was made to build 104 examples of the new Darl'mat 402. Production would consist of three sub-models: roadster, convertible and, the rarest of all, the coupé, of which only a handful were built.

The basis for all three versions included a chassis with independent front suspension and a live rear axle. Hydraulic drum brakes are fitted to all four wheels. Power comes from Peugeot's 1,999.6 cc overhead valve four-cylinder engine rated at 70 bhp mated to a four-speed Cotal electromagnetic transmission. The chassis were fabricated at the Peugeot facilities at Sochaux and were then shipped to Darl'mat, who installed the mechanical upgrades. From there they traveled to Pourtout's shop to be bodied in aluminum. With the bodies and interior trim installed, they were returned to the Darl'mat garage for their final touches. The completed 402 Darl'mat specials weighed in at 2,238 pounds. Production continued until the beginning of World War II in 1939.

The Darl'mat 402 coupé was a favorite at many concours d'élégance, wining prizes at Deauville in 1938 and in Paris that same year. One of Paulin's more radical designs, it's sleek and catlike, with an unusual round trunk, a heart-shaped faired-in license plate frame, a grille that slopes back and polished aluminum Art Deco air intake grills along the sides of the hood.

This car was brought to the United States some time in the 1950s and ended up in Nevada. At some point it was fitted with twin filler caps on the trunk and is believed to have run on the salt flats several times. The Darl'mat was later stored for almost 40 years until it was bought by collector Jim Patterson in 2000. When he acquired it, the Darl'mat was complete, but in pieces. Patterson had it fully restored before it debuted at Pebble Beach in 2004. However, he wasn't satisfied with the results and sent it to Canada to be restored again—this time by RM Restorations. Following the second restoration it won many prizes and remains in the Jim Patterson collection.

Emile Darl'mat continued working at his dealership until his death in 1970. The garage exists today in Paris and continues to represent the Peugeot Company.

–RA & DM

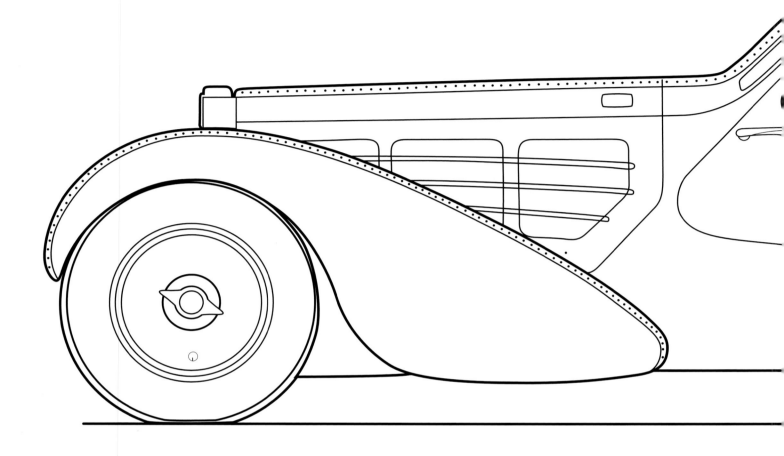

1936 Bugatti Type 57SC Atlantic

Ettore Bugatti pursued his own vision of automotive perfection. His cars were fast and, with very few exceptions, were possessed of uncommon beauty. He was joined in his motorcar mission by his son, Jean, who like his father, uncles and grandfather, had a superb eye for form and design.

Like virtually all manufacturers in the 1910s and '20s, Bugatti held but a rudimentary concept of streamlining and aerodynamics. The company's earliest attempt to redress wind resistance came in 1922 when a rounded radiator cowl and sharply tapered tail was fitted to each of the company's entries for the Strasbourg Grand Prix.

The following year, the cars were entered in the 200 mile race at Brooklands and the single-seaters for Indianapolis were also fitted with radiator cowls and tapered tails. However, in a break from the company's past practice, at the Grand Prix at Tours, Bugatti fielded a team of straight-eight-powered Type 32 racers with all enveloping, streamlined "tank" bodies.

Under the guidance of Jean Bugatti, the tank concept was revived in 1937 for the company's Le Mans effort with the Type 57 G chassis. Thanks to the low, wide and streamlined form, the Le Mans Bugatti was capable of very high

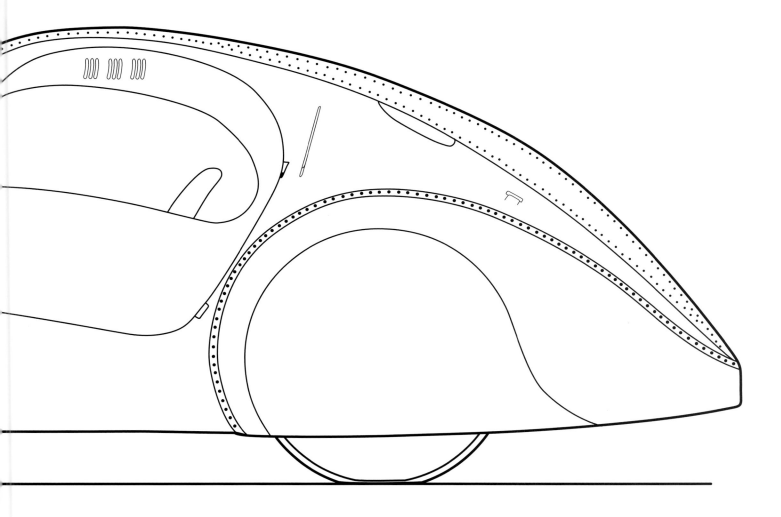

speeds. Wearing the number 2, for the 24 hour race the Le Mans Tank finished first overall driven by Jean-Pierre Wimille and Robert Benoist. This was a remarkable feat considering that it was the first Le Mans race for the Bugatti Tank as well as for Wimille. At Le Mans in 1939, with the race team now managed by Jean Bugatti, Wimille repeated his triumph with co-driver Veyron.

Although the Type 57 G was Bugatti's competition model, the road-going Type 57 had been introduced in 1933 as a high-performance chassis to serve as a platform for the finest and most modern custom coachwork. Under Jean Bugatti's leadership, the factory adopted a single-model policy and devoted all the factory's resources to the Type 57 and its variations. The model evolved

into the Type 57 S, which featured a much lower center of gravity and superior handling. To facilitate the lower chassis, the rear axle passed through the frame. The new Vee radiator was smaller and sleeker and better suited to modern aerodynamic styling.

The 57 S was powered by a 3,257cc double-overhead camshaft straight eight engine with a dry-sump oiling system and Scintilla Vertex magneto ignition. In supercharged SC form, the engine produced a potent 220 hp. With a wheelbase of 117.4 inches, the chassis was 12.6 inches shorter than that of the standard Type 57 chassis. The four-speed manual transmission sent sufficient power aft to the rear wheels to propel the elegant Bugatti to 125 mph.

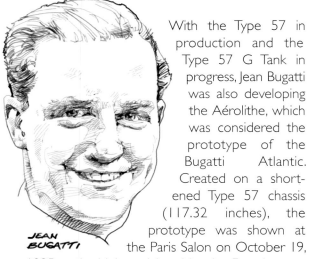

JEAN
BUGATTI

With the Type 57 in production and the Type 57 G Tank in progress, Jean Bugatti was also developing the Aérolithe, which was considered the prototype of the Bugatti Atlantic. Created on a shortened Type 57 chassis (117.32 inches), the prototype was shown at the Paris Salon on October 19, 1935, and widely acclaimed by the French automotive press. Unlike the later Atlantic, which was built on the lower Type 57 S chassis, the Aérolithe also used a flat-faced radiator, which raised the hood line and compromised the aerodynamics of the front-end styling. The headlights, however, were faired into the inside of the front fenders, unlike those on the Atlantic, which were raised and detached.

Much lore surrounds the material used to construct the body of the Aérolithe, although most evidence suggests that the car was made out of Elektron, the trademark name for a magnesium alloy. Other references mention an aluminum alloy, Duralumin. Both alloys are very difficult to work with and to weld, which is why rivets were used in the construction of the fenders and the roof section.

The Type 57 S Atlantic was introduced on the Bugatti stand at the Paris Salon in 1936. At a cost of 141,000 French francs (roughly $9,400), it was one of the most expensive cars at the show. At the factory, the striking new coupé was initially known as the "competition model," although it was ultimately called the Atlantic.

Universally considered Jean Bugatti's greatest design, the Atlantic's control surfaces are the synthesis of Bugatti streamlined styling. During the period of the model's gestation, Jean was running all aspects of the factory with his father as his advisor. As the chief designer, Jean was also personally responsible for the Atlantic's dramatic styling. Although there is no documented record of wind tunnel testing, the car was a stunning example of streamlined styling that also proved to have an extremely effective shape.

Of the three factory Atlantics, chassis 57.374 was built for Lord Phillippe de Rothschild and finished in a pale grey blue metallic with blue leather interior. Originally delivered as a Type 57 S, it was reportedly supercharged at the factory in 1939 and upgraded to 57 SC specifications. A short time after the modifications, Lord Rothschild damaged the engine.

The Rothschild car was subsequently stored in England until it was sold to Tip Turnard of London in 1941. In 1944, Rodney Clark of Continental Cars in Surrey acquired the car and, in turn, sold it to Robert Oliver, a wealthy American. The following year, Oliver had the car shipped to New York City and driven to his home in Los Angeles. Oliver returned the Atlantic to the factory in Molsheim in 1952 and performed a mechanical and cosmetic restoration. When the work was done, Oliver picked up the car and drove it to Turin, Italy, where he had the coachwork modified by Motto to enlarge the rear windows and install front and rear bumpers. After the car was repainted Bugatti Blue, it was used briefly in Europe, then crated and sent to Los Angeles, where it sat—still in its crate—until it was disinterred in 1970. Once resurrected, the Atlantic was displayed at the Briggs Cunningham Museum in Costa Mesa, California. Oliver took the car for one last ride following its revival and died shortly after.

Subsequent to Oliver's death, in 1971, the Atlantic was sent to auction at Sotheby's in Los Angeles, where it was acquired by Dr. Peter Williamson. Largely untouched for 30 years, shortly after the turn of the century, Williamson had the car comprehensively restored to its original specifications by Bugatti specialist Jim Stranberg. Shown at Pebble Beach in 2003, it won both its class and best of show.

– JAS, RA & DM

ATLANTIC

Châssis " Type 57 S" avec carrosserie "ATLANTIC"
2 places - 2 portes

VITESSE

Top: The Bugatti 57S with Atlantic coachwork as featured in a factory brochure from 1938.
Bottom: Bugatti's competition model, the aerodynamic 57G "Tank" winning Le Mans in 1937.

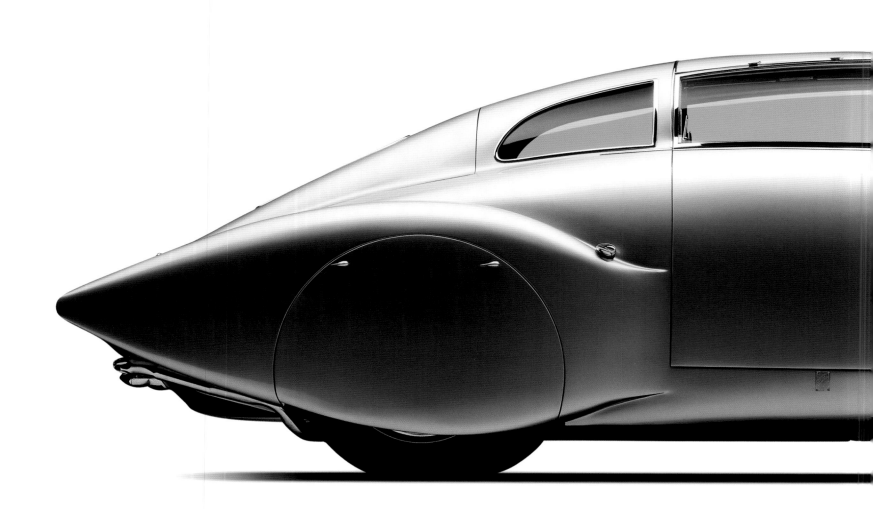

1937 DUBONNET HISPANO H-6C XENIA

Long, wide and massive, with a fuselage and cockpit clearly inspired by aircraft practice, the Dubonnet Hispano-Suiza evokes yesterday's vision of the future. Built in 1938, it was unlike anything on the roads of the day. It combined André Dubonnet's unique suspension, the pioneering aerodynamic design of Jean Andreau and the craftsmanship of Joseph Saoutchik's famed carrosserie.

Born in 1897, André Dubonnet was a member of the family of famous French aperitif makers of the same name. Growing up with wealth and privilege, he soon showed a keen interest in

engineering and design. Early in life he developed a passion for airplanes and, at the start of World War I, became a fighter pilot. Flying with the French Air Service's Stork Squadron, he was credited with five kills.

Once the war was over, his delight in speed and adventure turned to race cars. He became an accomplished racecar driver, and was a member of the victorious Duesenberg team (finishing fourth) in the 1921 French Grand Prix. Although he had driven the Duesenberg successfully, Hispano-Suiza was always his favored marque. Despite tire failure, he drove a Hispano

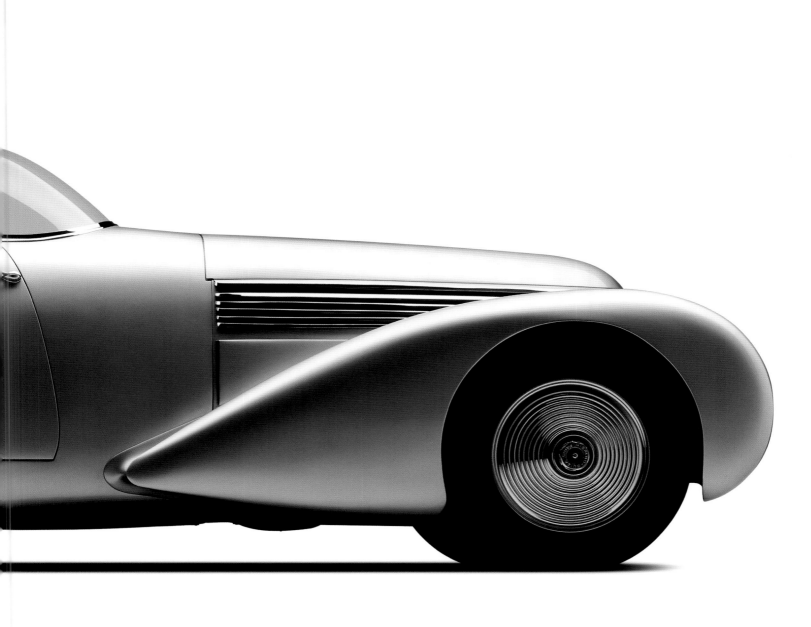

to a competitive sixth place in the grueling 1924 Targa Florio.

In addition to racing, Dubonnet had experimented with his own suspension design. To showcase the invention, he installed it in a prototype prepared specifically for publicity purposes. Drawing on his aviation background and racing experience for inspiration, he began sketching a design that would be built on the 1932 Hispano-Suiza H6B chassis which had been displayed at the Paris Salon. The chassis was extensively modified to incorporate his ideas. Dubonnet claimed that his "hyperflex suspension system would give it the suppleness of a cat" and used a "jumping cat" as his corporate logo.

When it came time to clothe his creation, Dubonnet commissioned Jean Andreau, a French expert in streamlined styling, to combine contemporary aerodynamic design and Dubonnet's own ideas. Andreau's creations were often so avant-garde that spectators were startled into wondering whether they were looking at a bird, a dolphin or an airplane. He strongly influenced the design of the automobiles of the era, but perhaps because his focus was theoretical, based upon his scientific and engineering background, he was not publicly recognized and never achieved great commercial success. Nevertheless, the design for the Dubonnet was clean, with simple lines, and it was presented to leading Paris coachbuilder Joseph Saoutchik to

JEAN ANDREAU

build the body. When Saoutchik was finished, the car looked completely unlike the flamboyant and chrome-laden confections for which he was known.

In fact, the car shows the influence of Dubonnet's experience as a pilot – the interior looks like an airplane cockpit, with curved Plexiglas side windows that pop out like gull wings. A new parallel opening door system was used as part of the aerodynamic design, and special attention was given to the undercarriage for clean air movement. This 1938 car was built to reach 125 mph, which rivaled any car of the time, and had a cutting edge four wheel independent suspension. The Xenia is important because of its ultra modern design and the incorporation of Andreau's aerodynamic styling.

Research confirms that the car was completed some time in 1938. Several years earlier, Dubonnet had married the beautiful young Xenia Johnson, but she died soon afterwards. Still grieving over her loss, he named the car Xenia, which did not sit well with his new wife.

Once World War II broke out in 1939, the Xenia was carefully hidden. It did not reappear until June 9, 1946, when it was photographed at the opening of the Saint Cloud Highway tunnel outside Paris.

Viewed today, the coachwork of the Dubonnet Xenia has the look of a contemporary prototype. In radical contrast to the designs of the time, all the body's features are fully enclosed in what is known as "envelope style." Although the appearance is very sleek, it was built on a high chassis and is a large and heavy car. Nevertheless, all the viewer sees in the futuristic design created by Andreau is speed and lightness. Today the car still stands as a milestone in aerodynamic styling.

In 1955, the car was owned by Raymond Aussibal of Paris, and then at some point in the 1960s it was purchased by Alain Balleret, president of the French Hispano-Suiza Club, who began its restoration. The Xenia then became the property of Mr. Charles Morse of Seattle, Washington who restored it and displayed it at Pebble Beach in 2000. Peter Mullin later added it to his collection, where it remains today.

– RA & DM

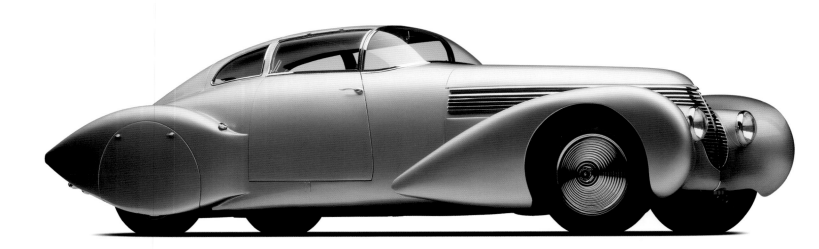

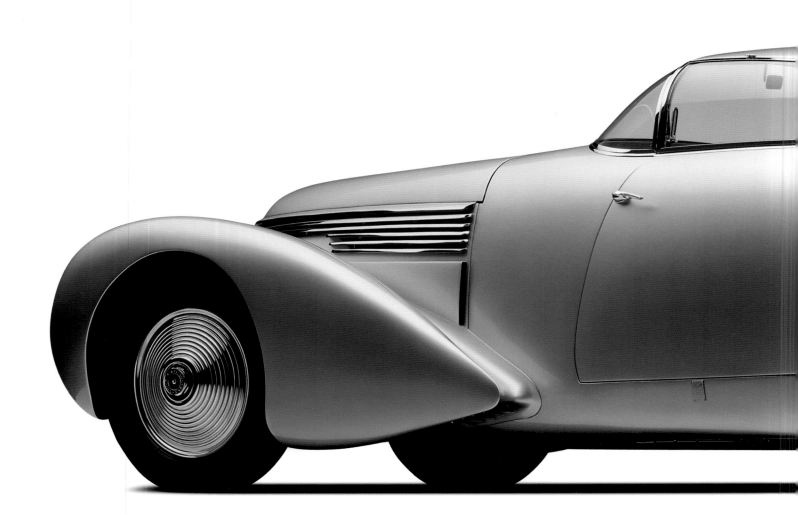

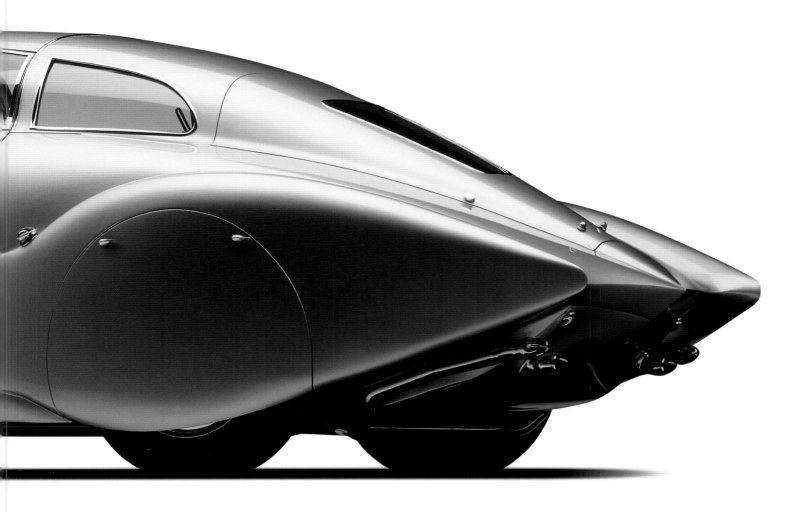

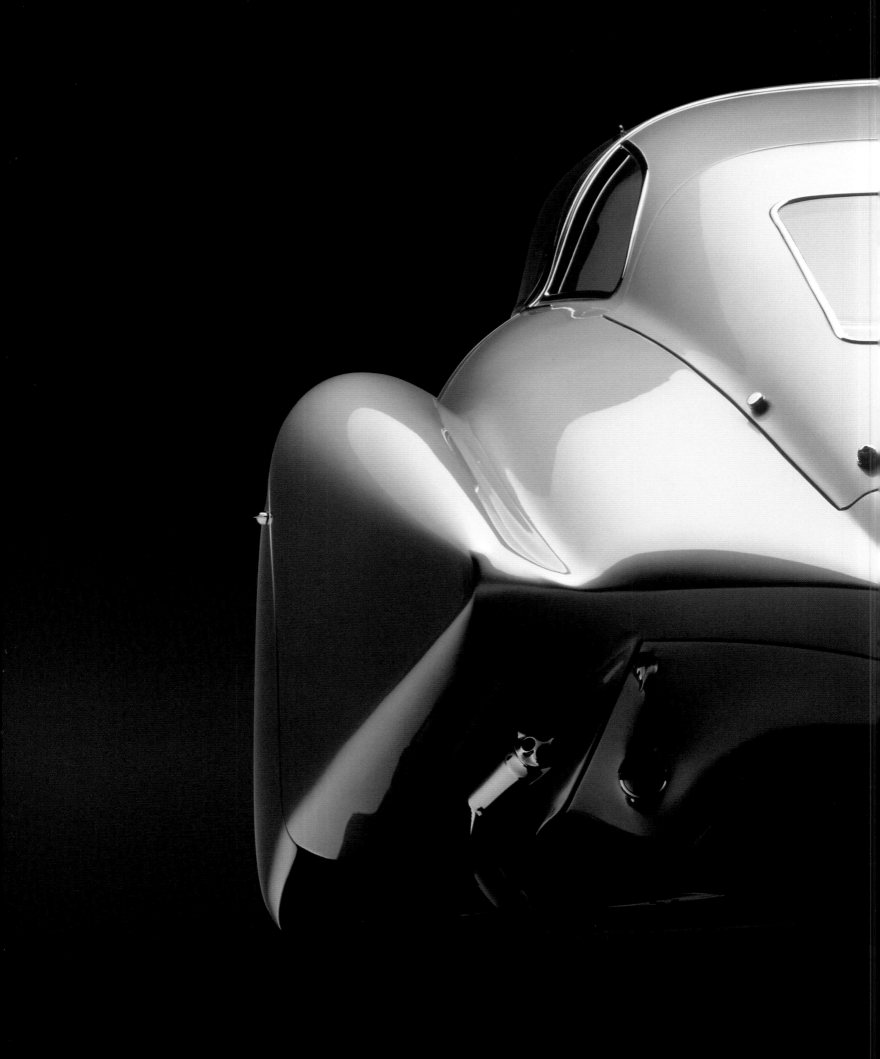

1937 DELAGE D8-120 S

In 1936, Louis Delage formed a new enterprise known as the Société Nouvelle des Automobiles Delage (SNAD), with fresh capital provided by the Delahaye company. One of his first ventures was the design of the D8-100 and D8-120 chassis that became enormously popular with carrossiers Letourneur & Marchand, Chapron, Pourtout, Saoutchik and others, who used it to launch some of their best work.

At a management meeting on November 5, 1936, it was decided that the company would build a prototype D8-120 chassis with a lowered suspension (known as "surbaissé") and an over-

bored (to 3.3-inches) 4.75-liter straight-eight engine. The suspension would make the car more maneuverable, the modified engine give sharper acceleration and the coachbuilders would follow a new set of body dimensions to create a smaller car. Compared to the standard D8-120 chassis, it was lower and lighter, with a narrower track, large wheels and a powerful engine. The prototype would be presented at the Paris Auto Salon of 1937.

Production was entrusted to Marcel Pourtout and his principal stylist, Georges Paulin. In March 1937, Louis Delage wrote to Pourtout, confirming his

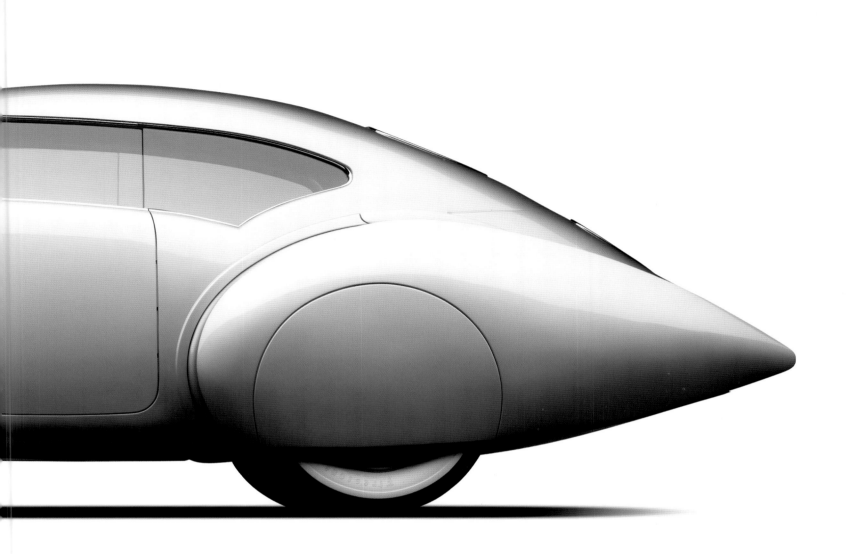

order for a "Conduite Interieur Sport," or sports sedan. He also advised Pourtout to "take great care in making this car, as this can be interesting for you as well as for us."

Pourtout replied three days later, saying that the grand plan would be ready by April 5. The original drawings by Paulin showed that he had created a sleek and aerodynamic masterpiece, and one of the earliest automobile shapes to be tested in a wind tunnel. Once the drawings were complete, Paulin created a scale wooden model which he tested at the wind tunnel at Meudon, near Paris. He then sent a full-scale wooden model to Meudon. Paulin followed the same steps to test the aerodynamic features of his next creation,

the Embiricos Bentley, which was also tested at the Vickers wind tunnel in Great Britain.

In less than seven months, the car went from concept to finished product, in time to be displayed at the Salon on October 7, 1937. The coachwork alone cost 31,200 francs and the chassis an additional 108,000 francs, making it an extremely expensive car which would cost roughly $92,000 today.

Louis Delage retained the car, chassis number 51620, for his personal use, and showed it at different concours in France until war started in 1939. It was sold in 1940 to a Mr. Penicaud, who stored it until fighting ended. During his ownership,

Mr. Penicaud brought his car to Joseph Saoutchik for repairs to damages caused by an accident. It was updated with a new grille, windshield and a one-piece rear window, replacing the original cat's-eyes.

MARCEL
POURTOUT

In 2002, Sam and Emily Mann bought the Delage. Mr. Mann conducted an exhaustive research effort that uncovered the original correspondence on the car, design drawings, build documents from the Pourtout archive and period photographs. Restoration was made easier by the fact that although the Delage had arrived in many pieces, it was, remarkably, 98-percent complete.

In contrast to the work of other contemporary designers, there are no chrome filets or external decorations on the body to emphasize the design. Rather, the continuous curves and tapers of the all-aluminum coachwork are allowed to speak for themselves. During its two-and-a-half year restoration, these smooth curves posed a challenge when the time came to apply the paint. To avoid seams along the roof line, two painters stood at opposite sides and simultaneously sprayed from one edge to another. The color was carefully chosen: a pearly silver with a small amount of metallic powder. In the light, the color reflects and highlights the lines of the car and the purity of the design. Curved lines repeat in all the elements of the Delage—fenders, wheels, windows and doors—opposing and complementing each other.

The rear end of the car tapers towards the center, emphasized by the newly-replaced cat's-eye window. The glass of the windshield is curved and wrapped, which was a significant technical feat for the time.

The interior of the car is simple. Seats are upholstered in Prussian blue leather, in a style known as waterfalls pleats, which start at the floor level, roll up the cushion and back and then down the rear. The headliner is gray wool, to match the exterior, and the dash is simple and functional.

Once finished, it was driven for 250 miles. With the throttle half down at 75 mph and holding firmly to the road, in Sam Mann's words, "it shifts smoothly and handles crisply and wants to fly."

It was shown for the first time at the 2005 Concours d'Elegance at Pebble Beach, which was celebrating the one hundred year anniversary of the Delage marque. Shimmering in the morning mist, this gorgeous car swept the field and went on to win First in Class and Best of Show. It was to be the fourth Best of Show trophy won by its owners.

In 2005, the Delage was awarded the Louis Vuitton Classic Concours Award, which is presented each year in Paris to a car chosen from among the winners of "Best of Show" prizes at the world's major concours d'élégance. It was displayed at the 2006 Retromobile exhibit in Paris and it remains in the collection of Sam and Emily Mann in New Jersey.

– RA & DM

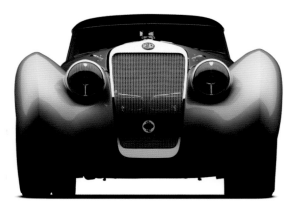

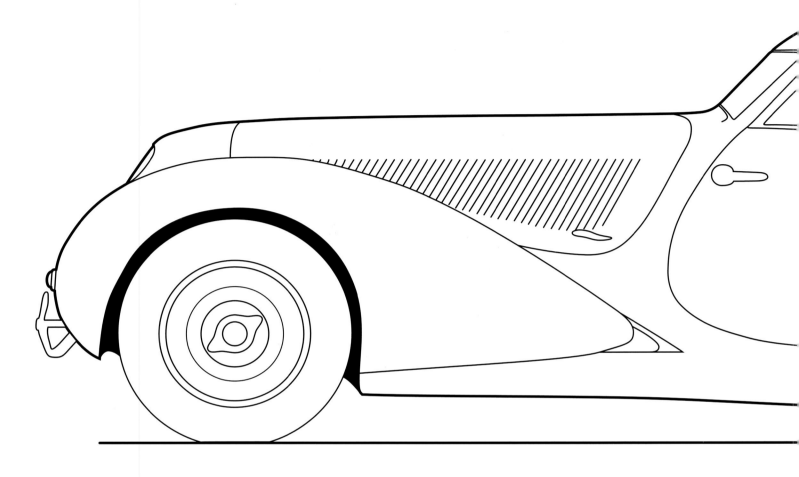

1938 BENTLEY 4 1/4 LITRE "EMBIRICOS"

It would be difficult to visualize a less likely background for an automotive designer than that of Georges Paulin. Born in 1902, the son of a market porter, Paulin was brought up in one of the tougher suburbs of Paris. From an early age, he revealed a prodigious talent for creative design and invention. However, his impoverished upbringing meant that his family could not afford higher education for the boy, and at age 14, he was forced to seek a living and trained as a dental technician.

Perpetually short of money, Paulin still kept inventing, and in 1931 filed his first patent, for a retractable top which eventually went into production as the Peugeot "Eclipse." This was at the urging of the Parisian Peugeot agent Emile Darl'mat, for whom Paulin also designed elegant roadsters and coupés on tuned Peugeot 302 chassis. These were constructed by coachbuilder Marcel Pourtout of Rueil-Malmaison, one of the swankier Parisian suburbs, who up to then had ploughed a solidly conservative course.

Paulin's designs were based on a profound knowledge of aerodynamics. Unlike his contemporaries, who modeled their concepts in clay or as wood or strap-iron "hammer forms," he

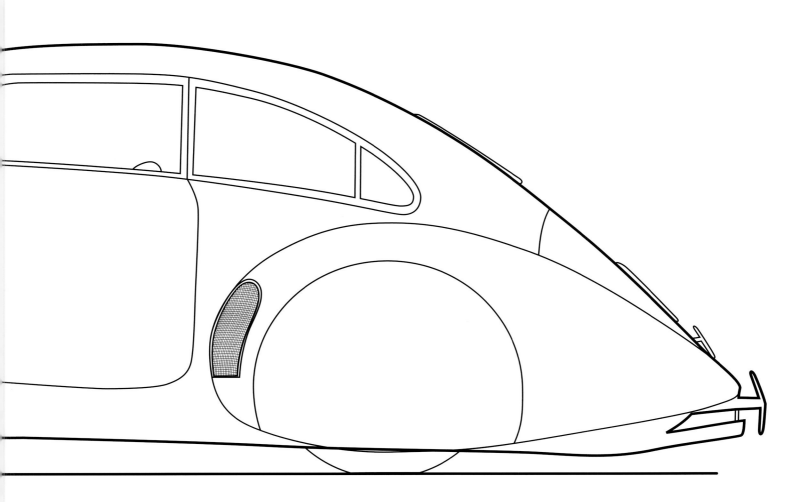

produced detailed full-scale lofting drawings from which Pourtout's skilled artisans produced his gloriously streamlined bodies.

In 1938, Paulin designed and Pourtout built two masterful high-speed closed four-seater coupés, one commissioned by Louis Delage on the prototype Delage D8-120S chassis, the other on an LE-series 4 1/4 Litre Overdrive Derby Bentley chassis.

According to historian Richard Adatto, the Bentley was commissioned for Greek shipping magnate André Embiricos, not his cousin Nico, who is usually claimed as its owner. Wind-tunnel tests of a scale model attracted the attention of Rolls-Royce, which was anxious to produce a

new Bentley model suitable for the high-speed roads that were being built in Europe.

Rolls-Royce works manager Ernest Hives knew something about the value of reducing head resistance, having achieved 101 mph at the wheel of a single-seat Silver Ghost at Brooklands before World War I. The test results of the streamlined Bentley were so impressive that Rolls-Royce invited Paulin to Derby and drew up a contract securing the exclusive rights to his services as a designer and aerodynamicist. "Georges Paulin," remarked Hives, "is twenty to thirty years ahead in terms of aerodynamics."

Walter Sleator, head of the Parisian Rolls-Royce retailers Franco-Britannic Autos, was charged

GEORGES
PAULIN

with maintaining a close liaison with Paulin during the construction of the new Bentley, which was regarded as essentially the prototype for the Mk V 4 1/4-liter planned for the 1940 season.

While bodies with token streamlining had previously been built on Bentley chassis, the iconic Bentley radiator had always stood bluff at the car's prow. Paulin's design concealed the radiator behind a streamlined cowl, with only the winged "B" badge revealing the car's identity. The flowing teardrop wings were reminiscent of contemporary aircraft practice, with the rear wheels concealed behind spats. Headlamps, door-handles, hinges and window frames were flush-fitting and a much larger than standard undertray faired in the belly of the car and the tail of the body tapered smoothly to a point beneath twin triangular rear windows. The inner edges of the rear wings curved gently inwards and surely guided the air flow to create an invisible "tail cone" behind the car to eliminate drag-inducing eddies.

Paulin appreciated that clean lines were not the only factor in achieving high speed, and made extensive use of Duralumin to cut the weight to 3,475 lb, some 340 pounds lighter than the normal 4 1/4-liter. Special domed pistons raised the compression ratio to 8:1 (standard was 6.5:1) and larger-than-usual SU-type carburetors with oil-controlled dashpots to minimize flat spots were fitted. Performance was further enhanced by an overdrive gearbox with a taller 2.87:1 final drive ratio. So equipped, the streamlined Bentley had a theoretical maximum speed of 120 mph — a 1939 Brooklands lap speed of 114 mph by recordbreaker George Eyston suggests it was even quicker. With only approximately a dozen genuine 100 mph cars in production in Europe at the time, the new Bentley's performance was remarkable.

Soon after it was completed, it was given an extended 1,000-mile road test from central Paris to Germany and back by racing driver and Autocar staffer John Dugdale. Fuelled with high-octane Azur fuel, at one stage the streamlined car covered 64 miles in 50 minutes — an impressive average of over 76 mph — and recorded a speed of over 120 mph on the autobahn in Germany.

"This," said Dugdale, "is a new aspect of motoring; it is the nearest thing to flying."

But he noted that the slippery shape of the Paulin Bentley meant that head resistance played little part in slowing from speed, so special steel-lined aluminum brake drums were used that gave more powerful braking.

The only real drawback, it seems, was restricted headroom in the rear seats. Otherwise, Dugdale found that the car, with a cruising speed of 110 mph, a fuel consumption of 25 miles per US gallon at 80 mph and "Bentley standards of silence and roadholding" was both "practical and remarkably fast" as a touring car.

Sadly, Embiricos was killed in a flying accident in 1939 and had little time to enjoy his car. Subsequently, Paulin applied the general principles of his streamline Bentley to a Vanvooren-bodied "Corniche" four-door saloon designed in conjunction with Ivan Evernden of Rolls-Royce and intended as a production body for the new Mk V chassis. However, an extended trunk and greater rear headroom compromised its lines. In any case, that body was destroyed by a bomb while in Vanvooren's workshop, and the four or five "Corniche" bodies under construction at the start of the war were lost.

Soon after the fall of France in 1940, Paulin was recruited by the British secret service MI6 — along with coachbuilder friend Jacques Kellner — to work against the German occupiers in one of the first Resistance networks, "Alibi." Kellner and Paulin were denounced to the Gestapo in 1942 and executed by firing squad.

But his glorious "streamline" Bentley lived on. It performed with honor in the first three post-war Le Mans 24-hour races (it came a more than creditable 6th in 1949 and, after the 1951 race, when it finished an unclassified 22nd, its owner Soltan Hay took it to Montlhéry and put 106 miles into the hour). It was a profound influence on the iconic Bentley Continental of 1952 and, after changing hands among enlightened enthusiasts, today is numbered among the rare vintages that comprise the collection of California winemaker Arturo Keller.

– DBW

The Embiricos Bentley was captured during a roadside stop for fuel in 1938. With its fared-in headlamps, sloping grille and raked V-windshields, it looks significantly more modern than the car behind.

George Paulin did what no designer had ever done to a Bentley—he tilted the grille back and covered it with a false nose for reduced aerodynamic drag.

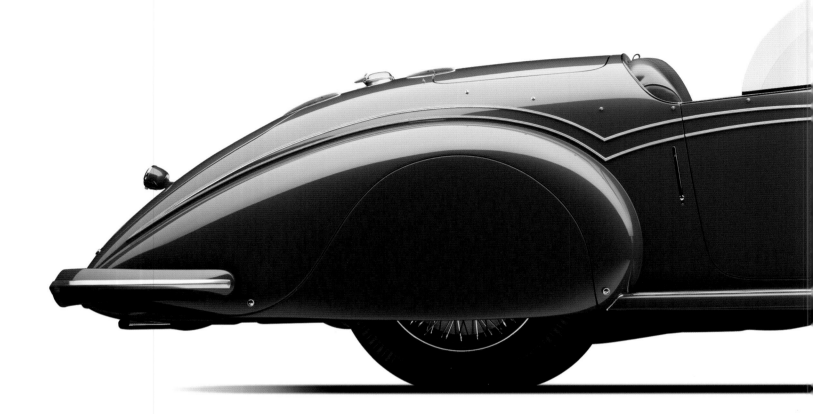

1938 ALFA ROMEO 8C-2900B

Long or short chassis, for racing or for the road, the 8C-2900 Alfa Romeo is among the most coveted of all automobiles. Bodied by Alfa Romeo, Touring, Pinin Farina and Stabilimenti Farina, many also consider it among the most beautiful cars of any era.

The 2.9 was the work of former Fiat engineer Vittorio Jano, who was lured to Milan to join Alfa Romeo. There he was responsible for the P2 and P3 (Tipo B) Grand Prix cars, as well as the 6C 1500, 6C 1750, 8C 2300 and 6C 2300. Although the first 6Cs were single-cams, Jano soon adopted the twin cam format and added

supercharging to make the sports and racing cars formidable competitors. With bodies usually by Zagato or Touring, the cars were attractive, although there was nothing revolutionary about them in terms of styling, with blunt radiator grilles, narrow cockpits and either swept or cycle fenders. Underneath the coachwork, a pair of cross-braced frame rails joined a pair of leaf-spring live axles with mechanical drum brakes on all four wheels.

The 8C 2900's impressive resume includes four wins in the Mille Miglia and two victories in the 24 Hours of Spa, not to mention countless

triumphs in other contests of speed and stamina on several continents.

At a time when many automobiles still relied on side valves and solid axles front and rear, the 8C-2900B was fitted with four-wheel independent suspension. The engine was Alfa's competition-proven double-overhead camshaft straight-eight fitted with twin-stage supercharging. Even in road-trim, output was 180 bhp. In higher tune, 220 bhp and more was easily possible. Before World War II, there was no sports car capable of higher speeds or better road holding.

The first public showing for the new Alfa Romeo sports car came in Autumn 1935 at the Paris show, where an 8C 2900A was shown with an Alfa Romeo spider body. Several body styles followed, but early on it became clear that Touring was the favored coachbuilder, offering spiders on both long and short chassis and a lovely berlinetta on the longer wheelbase.

Touring had started like most other companies, by using wooden framework to which metal panels were attached. The company's initial designs were very upright and conventional for the day, although finished to a very high standard. Drawbacks to the traditional coachbuilding methods included heavy weight and lack of chassis or body rigidity. As the chassis and body frames moved, the steel or aluminum body panels flexed and both the metal and the paint would craze and ultimately crack.

Touring's Felice Bianchi Anderloni sought to overcome these liabilities by obtaining a license to use the French Weyman method, which retained a wooden body frame, but replaced most of the metal panels with a stretched leather cloth or vinyl fabric. These bodies were lighter and the fabric would give as the frames flexed. However, complex curves simply weren't possible because of the use of the fabric panels.

As early as 1931, Anderloni had been studying ways to reduce turbulence in the open sports and racing cars his company was building. With time, radiators were tilted back, windshields were raked and fenders became more flowing and less upright and offered less obstruction to the air flowing past. Tool boxes, luggage compartments and the connections between running boards and fenders also became more integrated as Touring's designers attempted to smooth airflow.

The real breakthrough for Touring came in 1937 with the patented Superleggera method of construction, using a series of small diameter steel tubes bent and welded together to form a bird cage frame, which was welded to the chassis. Light alloy or steel panels were formed and positioned over the framework, with felt padding to prevent direct contact — and therefore electrolytic reaction — between the aluminum and steel. The resulting bodies were quite rigid and substantially lighter than contemporary wood-framed coachwork. Although the concept was similar to that used with the Weyman method, voluptuous curves were now possible.

With the advent of Superleggera construction, Touring's styling took a leap forward as it began to integrate the rear fenders into the main fuselage section of the car. The front fenders remained separate forms, but were much more streamlined shapes. The effect was startling and extremely attractive, with the Berlinettas (coupés) and spiders (roadsters) built on the sophisticated 8C-2900B chassis, perhaps the most beautiful cars of their — or any other — era.

Although not necessarily aerodynamic by modern standards, the Grand Tourismo 2.9 Alfas by Touring were clearly proponents of clean, streamlined design. Compared to coachwork of many of their contemporary carrozerrie, the company's work was extremely modern.

By most counts, fewer than 40 8C-2900s were built. Touring was responsible for approximately 23, of which 17 were spiders on either the long or short chassis with one very streamlined coupe built for Le Mans 1938. Car 412022 is a long-wheelbase chassis sent to Touring for a spider body. 2.9 authority Simon Moore believes that the car was shipped to England for the 1938 London Motor Show. For the duration of the war, it was stored by UK Alfa Romeo importer Thompson and Taylor. Subsequently, it passed through several UK owners, during which time the rear fenders and tail were apparently modified. After sojourns in several major Alfa Romeo collections, enthusiast and racecar constructor Peter Agg acquired it in the 1980s and ran it in the Mille Miglia.

By 1985, it was in the hands of American collector John Mozart who retained it for several years before it was acquired by a Japanese collector who sent it to Dino Cognolato in Italy, who restored the rear body to the original shape and restored the car in red with a red interior. The car subsequently returned to the United States for collector William E. "Chip" Connor, II, who had Bob Mosier restore 412022 to its original gray livery. Since completion, Connor has presented the car at the Pebble Beach Concours d'Elegance and the "Quail Motorsport Gathering," and has driven it in the 2003 and 2005 Alfa Tours of the Rockies.

— JAS

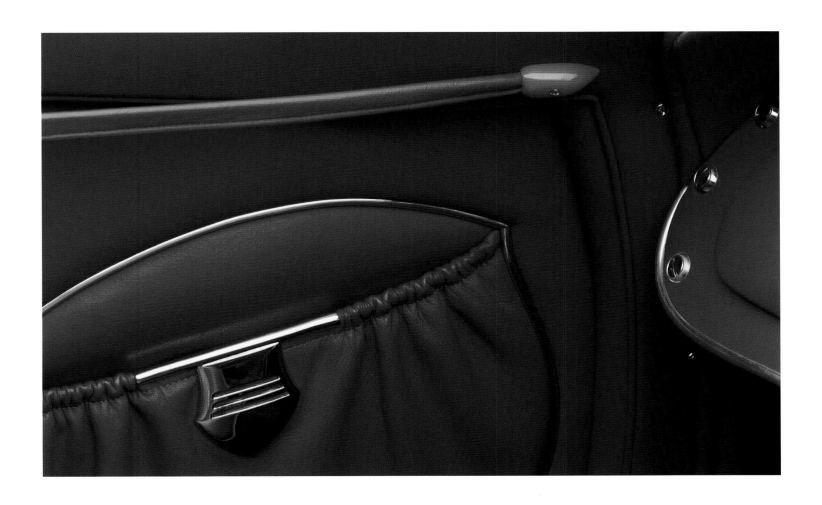

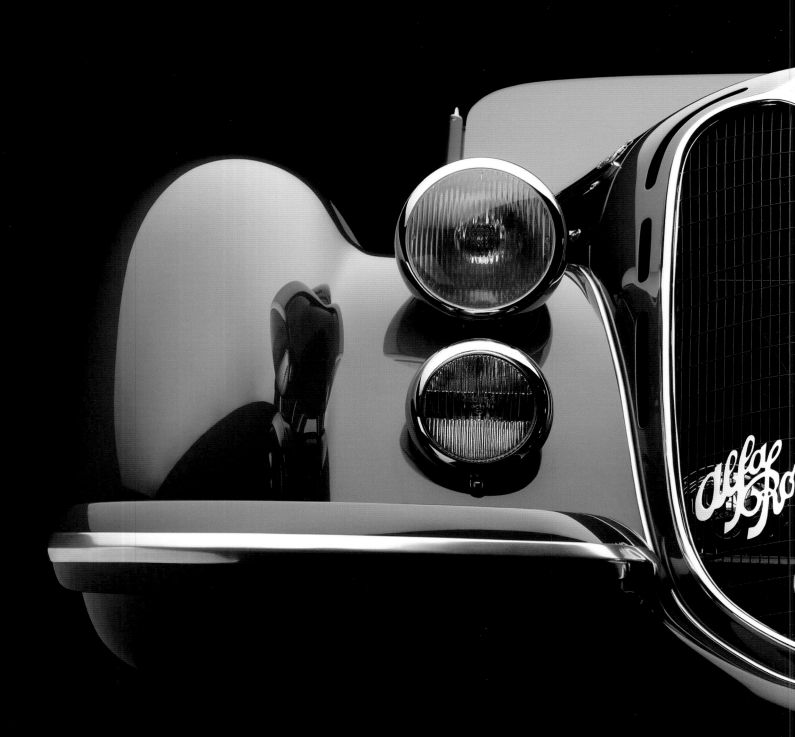

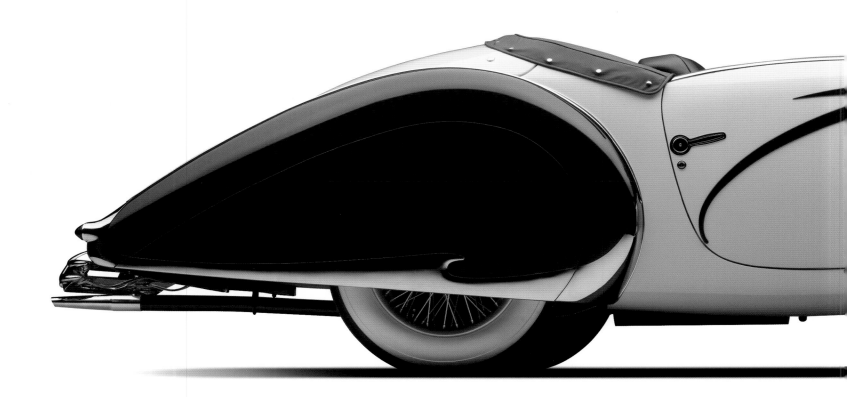

1938 DARRACQ/TALBOT-LAGO T150-C

One of the most sophisticated and well-balanced cabriolets ever bodied by Figoni & Falaschi is the 1938 Talbot-Lago T150-C-Lago Spéciale. Its streamlined styling starts at the leading edge of the front fender and continues through to the tapered tail that conceals the convertible top. To add to the open-air experience, the V-shaped windscreens fold down. The dashboard is also V-shaped and, in traditional Figoni style, uses elegant woodwork.

According to Joseph Figoni's son, Claude, it is the only Talbot-Lago cabriolet with fully enclosed pontoon fenders bodied by Figoni and Falaschi. This single car represents the peak of aesthetic

French design during the 1930s and is considered by many to be the most beautiful convertible in the world. Like many designs of the period, it was styled to look modern and fast and not based on aerodynamic theory.

Created on a standard wheelbase of 2.95 meters (116.142 inches), this T150-C Talbot model was designated "Lago Spéciale." However, because it was built for export, it was badged as a Darracq, which was a sister company to Talbot-Lago.

The T150-C is powered by a four liter, overhead valve, in-line six-cylinder engine rated at 140 hp. Fuel enters the hemispherically-shaped combustion

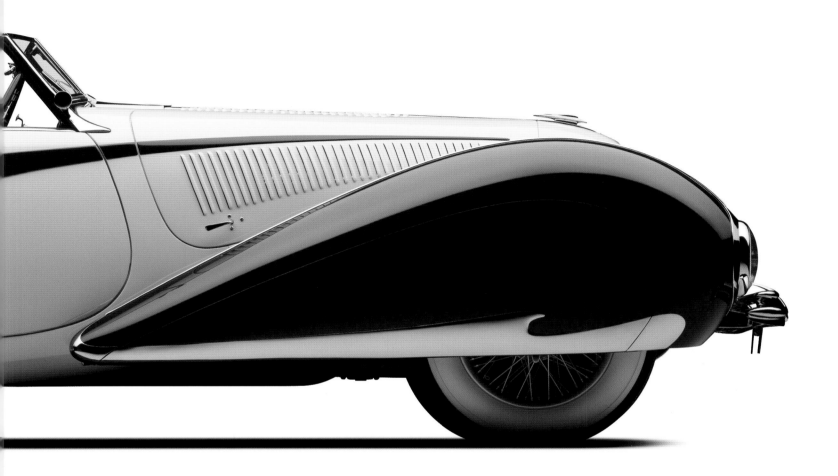

chambers courtesy of a trio of Zenith Stromberg EX32 carburetors mounted on individual intake manifolds equipped with both balance tubes and pre-heat tubes. A cast iron exhaust manifold is fitted to the other side of the cross-flow cylinder head. Power is transmitted to the rear axle via a four-speed Wilson pre-selector transmission.

Front suspension is independent by transverse leaf springs, with a live rear axle supported by semi-elliptical leaf springs and damped by Houdaille shock absorbers. Drum brakes are fitted inside all four center lock wire wheels. The completed car weighs 2,190 pounds and is capable of a top speed of 99.4 mph.

According to the Figoni archives, the original owner of chassis 90019 was the Portuguese Count of Covilhã, Júlio Anahory de Quental Calheiros. During World War II, the car remained hidden in Portugal while the family moved to Brazil to weather the conflict. When the war ended, the car was shipped to Brazil and remained there until the family brought it back to Portugal in 1948. After the count and countess died, it was kept at the family's tire factory in Famalicão, Covilhã, lovingly polished by the chauffeur. Finally, in 1975 the count's daughter sold it to Michel Poberejsky, who during the 1950s raced Ferraris and other marques using the pseudonym "Mike Sparken."

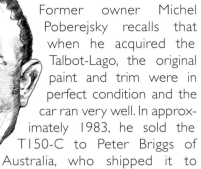

JOSEPH
FIGONI

Former owner Michel Poberejsky recalls that when he acquired the Talbot-Lago, the original paint and trim were in perfect condition and the car ran very well. In approximately 1983, he sold the T150-C to Peter Briggs of Australia, who shipped it to England and then to Paris for restoration at the Le Coq restoration shop. Resplendent in fresh paint, in 1985 the elegant cabriolet was displayed on the Le Coq stand at Retromobile in Paris.

In 1987, the car was purchased at auction and then shipped to Florida. It remained under the same ownership until 2000, when it was sold to J. Williard Marriott, Jr. After careful research and a complete restoration, it was shown at the Pebble Beach Concours d'Elegance in 2006 where it received the prestigious French Cup. Later in the year, it was awarded Best of Show at the Radnor Hunt Concours. It remains in the J. Williard Marriott, Jr. collection.

– RA & DM

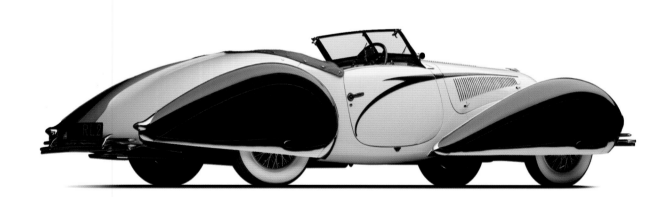

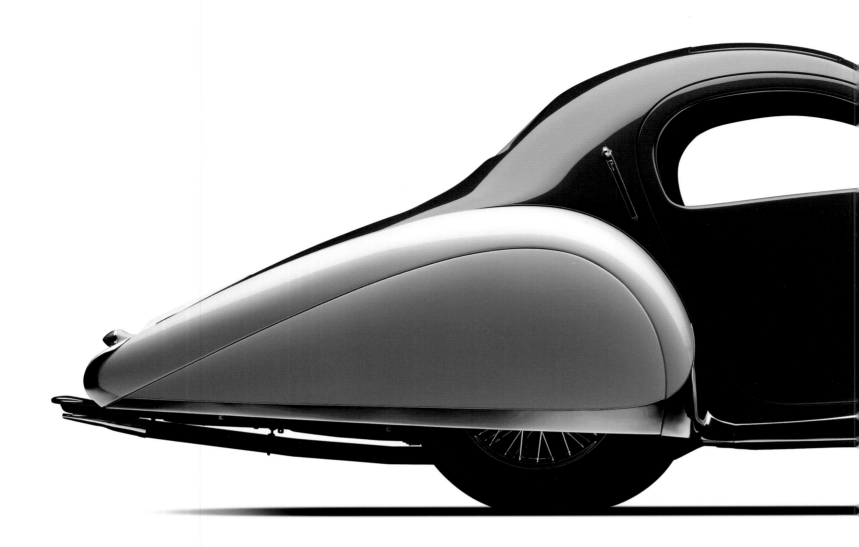

1938 TALBOT-LAGO T150-C-SS

A full 70 years after conception, any one of Figoni & Falaschi's voluptuous teardrop coupés will stop any viewer in his tracks. The teardrop shape that is echoed in the roofline and fender shapes is clear proof that this body style represents Joseph Figoni's masterwork.

Without relying on wind tunnel testing or advanced engineering, Figoni used his knowledge of aviation and artistic talents to create this unique coachwork. Strother McMinn, a well known stylist, instructor at the Art Center College of Design and respected former chief honorary judge of the Pebble Beach Concours

d'Elegance, remembered a conversation with Figoni, who waved his tough, metalworker's hands through the air in a sinuous curve and exclaimed, "I have always loved the streamline!" Thus with a gesture far more expressive than words, he very simply proclaimed his passion for a tactile craftsmanship that created graceful, compelling and artfully fluid forms.

Although Figoni & Falaschi built approximately 16 teardrop coupés, Chassis 90104 is one of three examples of the Jeancart style on the Talbot-Lago T-150C chassis. The styling was slightly modified according to the Figoni archive to honor original

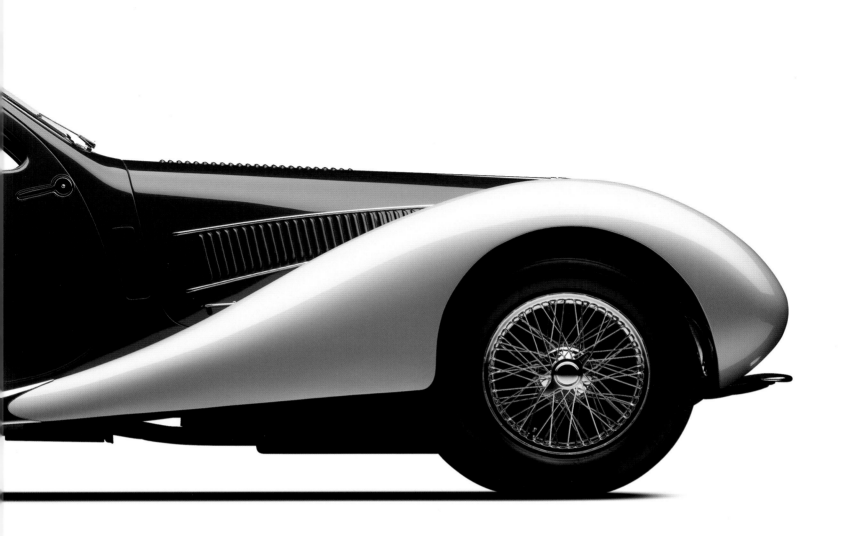

buyer, M. Jeancart's request for more interior room. The driver's seat was pushed back, reducing the trunk space so much that the spare tire would no longer fit. The car was ordered with a sunroof and the chassis and engine hood were reinforced.

Its design is classic Figoni: the windshield slopes back and the roofline rolls into a soft notchback that ends in a taper with cat's-eye rear windows. The front fenders arch over the wheels holding tightly to the body and connect to the rear fenders which pick up the teardrop shapes. The rear wheels are covered to lower the aerodynamic resistance of the car. To further reduce aerodynamic drag, the hardware and headlights are flush to the body.

Dr. Fernand Masquéfa, a prominent plantation owner and car enthusiast in Algeria, ordered the car from Figoni in 1938. It was exported through Portuguese importer S.A.V.A.H. to the Talbot-Lago concessionaire in Oran, Algeria. Masquéfa used the car to drive to and from his orange groves in Algeria and Morocco, at a time when both countries were French colonies. Bowling along the rough roads was an adventure and it is a testament to the car's versatility and strength that Dr. Masquéfa was able to drive it for 40 years. Apparently, he also found time to privately enter it in races and rallies. There are unconfirmed reports that the car participated in the Rally of Algiers, the Rally of Morocco, the Grand Prix de Bône, and the Grand Prix of Algeria.

The quality and beauty of the Talbot-Lago exercised a powerful charm on Dr. Masquéfa, who kept the car for most of its life. Long after its original purchase, automotive enthusiast Jean-François du Montant discovered that Dr. Masquéfa still kept his beloved possession at one of his orange plantations. All through the late '70s, he made repeated offers to buy the car. In 1980, Dr. Masquéfa sent it to a Mercedes garage in Casablanca for restoration. The following year, he finally lost interest in the car and sold it to du Montant and Yves René Joseph for $13,000 U.S. dollars. While the coachwork and interior fittings showed some wear, it was in excellent running condition. Before buying the car, du Montant took it for a test drive without the hood or doors attached. "I thought the Wilson gearbox was slipping," he explained, "until I realized with pleasure that I was spinning the wheels and the tires were smoking due to the magnificent power of the engine."

In 1985, with the car appreciating in value, it was sold to Swiss dealer Jean-Pierre Schindelholz, who performed a ground-up restoration from 1990 to 1992. It re-emerged at the 1992 Concours d'Elegance Louis Vuitton in Zurich and at the Concours d'Elegance Louis Vuitton Bagatelle in Paris. At both events it won Best of Show.

On the strength of its European success, in 1993 the car was invited for display at the Pebble Beach Concours d'Elegance. The following year it

was purchased by Lukas Hüni of Switzerland, and then in April, 1995, it was sold to William E. "Chip" Connor, II, who had seen and admired it at Pebble Beach.

Once the engine had been reworked in the United Kingdom, the Talbot-Lago was sent to be restored in Inglewood, California. Careful scrutiny was paid to every detail to ensure that the car was returned to its original condition. During the course of the restoration, extensive research was conducted and Connor consulted the designer's son, Claude Figoni, on the original production specifications and color scheme. Based on information found in the company's archives, the car is now painted in its original radiant colors of marine blue and luminescent gray.

In 1997, the Talbot-Lago T-150C-SS was invited to be entered in the 47th annual Pebble Beach Concours d'Elegance. When the show was over, it had won First in Class and Best of show.

The teardrop coupe has continued its winning show history. In 1998, it won the Cartier Style et Luxe trophy at the Goodwood Festival of Speed in England and it was awarded the Christie's trophy at the 1998 Louis Vuitton Concours held at the Hurlingham Club in London on June 6, 1998.

This inspired example of Joseph Figoni's craft remains an important part of Chip Connor's collection.

– RA & DM

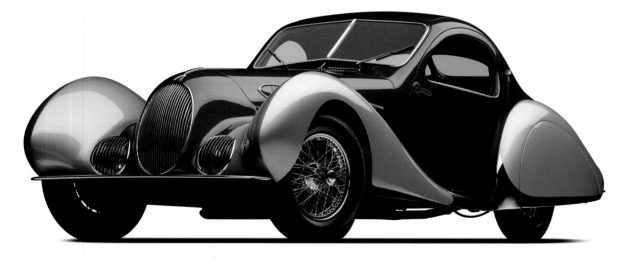

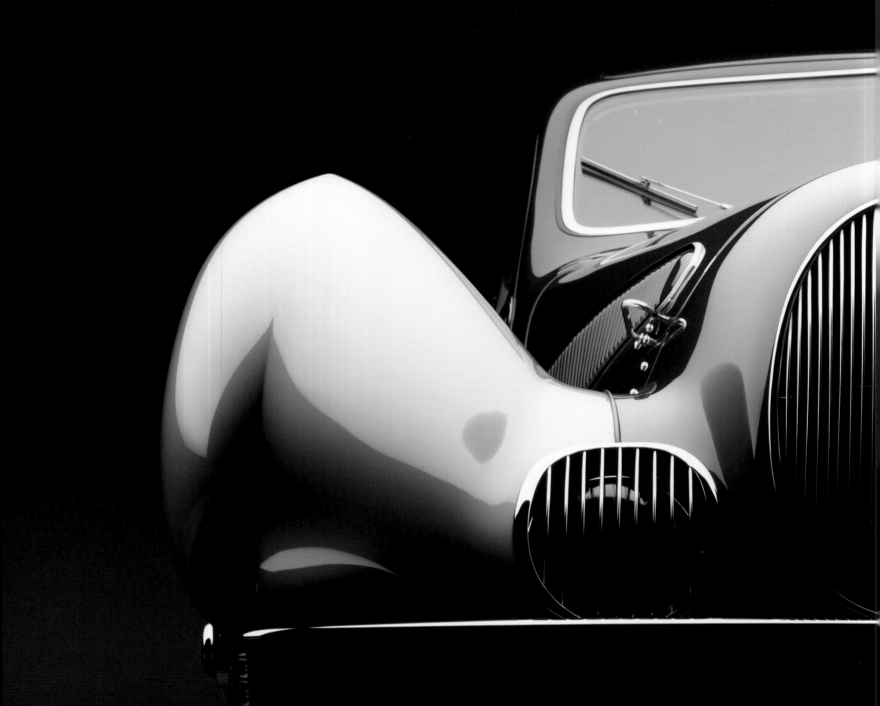

1939 DELAHAYE TYPE 165

For the French exhibit at the 1939 New York World's Fair, Delahaye turned to Figoni & Falaschi for the coachwork for its Type 165. By 1939, the United States was emerging from the Great Depression and the public was ready for optimism. In its official guide book, the Fair expressed its lofty goals as "Building the World of Tomorrow with the Tools of Today" and "The Interdependence of Men and Nations." The Fair was a huge success and although war broke out in Europe in September 1939, the Fair was extended into 1940. For the first time, the public was able to see very advanced designs for auto-mobiles, trains and boats. They accepted that

these fast streamlined models would become part of their daily lives.

The Delahaye destined for the Fair's French Pavilion was modeled after the Paris Salon car of 1938. However, the company faced a struggle to finish the Type 165 in time to ship it to New York for the Fair's official opening. Figoni & Falaschi alone invested 2,100 hours in the construction and finishing of the body frame, body panels and interior. In the end, the car had to be shipped before the engine was completed. The public could look at the interior through a cutout in the engine hood and admire the

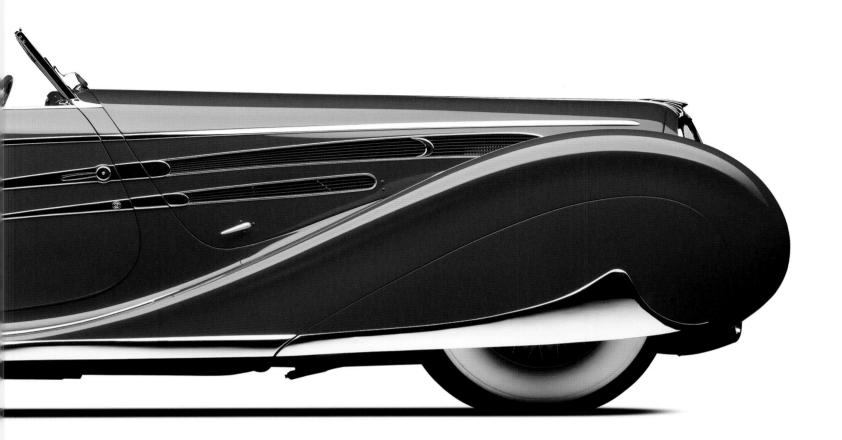

firewall and engine turned valve covers, which made for a showy display.

This car, chassis 60744, is a classic example of Joseph Figoni's love of streamlined designs. His son Claude recalls his father's habit of sculpting his maquettes in modeling clay, and explaining, "It is necessary to pay meticulous attention to the behavior of the wisps of air that flow between the wheel covers and the hood, and then lower their profile to reduce the wind resistance of the headlights. You must also pay attention to the curve of the hood." Figoni kept a model of the Couzinet Arc-en-Ciel airplane in his office and used its aerodynamic pontoons and sleek lines for inspiration. He was able also to look at unattractive but effective commercial aero-dynamic designs and turn them into unique and elegant shapes that were highly marketable.

Chassis 60744 received a cabriolet body, and featured fully-enclosed front and rear pontoon fenders, a roll-down windshield and a disappearing top, all of which allowed the car to go faster. The result was a car that curved voluptuously from front to back in teardrop style. Unlike many of his contemporary designs, Joseph Figoni styled the car without excessive ornamentation. Painted bright red, the gorgeous streamlined Figoni & Falaschi cabriolet was an immediate success at the World's Fair and drew large crowds and much media attention. Along with the Firestone-built Phantom Corsair, the Delahaye was the star of the show.

In 1981, collector Jim Hull was at Laguna Seca for the Monterey Historic Races when he met a couple who told him about an amazing Delahaye in California's Central Valley. Jim was eventually able to locate the car which belonged to a tow truck driver in Fresno. After four years of dialogue, a deal was made for the car. Jim and his partner, Peter Mullin, purchased the car in 1985. That same year, the partners also arranged to purchase the original V-12 engine from Count Dunhoff in Germany, who had bought it more than a decade earlier.

Jim and Peter's goal was to complete the restoration in time for the car's fiftieth anniversary in 1989. Due to many missing engine parts, the restoration was delayed and the car wasn't finished until 1992. It debuted at the Pebble Beach Concours in August of that year, where it won First in Class. Since then, the Delahaye has been shown around the world with great success. Its most recent triumph was another class win at the 2006 Pebble Beach Concours d'Elegance. It is now in the Peter Mullin collection of French streamlined cars.

– RA & DM

"Arc-en-ciel"
COUZINET 70

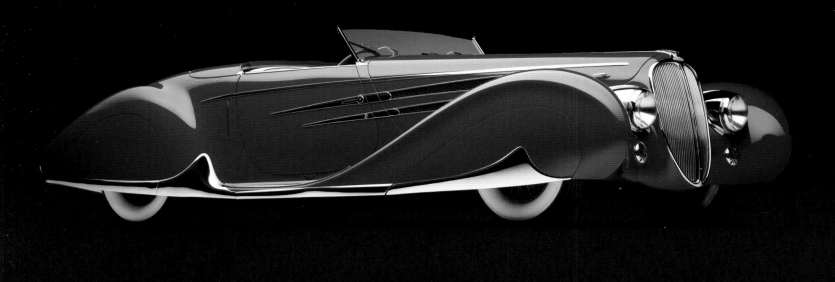

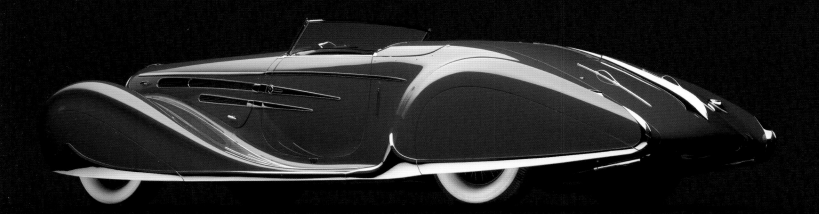

1948 TATRA T87

A list of owners including Egypt's King Farouk, racing driver Elizabeth Junek and author John Steinbeck, as well as heads of church and state would suggest a powerful, exotic and extravagant automobile. In the case of the Tatra T87, it was neither unusually powerful nor outrageously expensive. However, it was certainly exotic, from exterior design to the engineering and mechanical specifications.

Tatra approached automobiles differently than most other companies. The alternative approach was due to Austrian automobile designer Hans Ledwinka, who had worked under automotive

and aircraft pioneer Edmund Rumpler at Nesselsdorfer Waggonfabrik, which evolved into Tatra. He left the company twice for other employment; both times he was lured back. When he returned from Steyr in 1921, he promptly conceived and prepared a revolutionary people's car for production. The twin-cylinder, horizontally-opposed air-cooled engine was mounted up front and a rigid tube that served as a backbone chassis linked the integral engine/transmission casting and the final drive unit. A fully independent swing axle suspension did much to keep the wheels in contact with the brutally rough roads of newly-formed Czechoslovakia.

The T11, as the new car was called, proved extremely rugged and reliable. It also set a pattern of backbone chassis and independent suspension for Tatra. After 3,540 examples had been completed in 1926, the T11 was followed by the T12, which differed primarily by having four-wheel brakes, instead of its predecessor's rear brakes only. When production ceased in 1933, 7,525 examples of the T12 had been completed.

Meanwhile, Ledwinka and Tatra design engineer Erich Übelacker started experiments using a swing-axle-equipped backbone frame with a rear-mounted air-cooled twin in 1930. The initial prototype used a conventional body, but the V570 that followed was fitted with a much more

modern body design with a short nose, raked windshield and curved roof tapering into a fastback rear deck.

Although the V570 never saw production, it was a useful exercise in defining a new Tatra design philosophy. Like the prototype, Tatras of the future would feature the rear-engine layout which eliminated a driveshaft tunnel and allowed a more comfortable passenger compartment positioned fully within the wheel base. The revised boxed backbone chassis proved to be an ideal platform for the new science of streamlining that was being pioneered by airplane and Zeppelin designer Paul Jaray. A relatively short front was combined with a roofline sloping

HANS
LEDWINKA

into a long fastback tail. When integrated fenders and a full undertray were added, wind resistance was dramatically reduced and, as a result, a relatively modest power plant was able to achieve excellent performance and lower fuel consumption. A rear dorsal fin ensured stability.

Tatra's new design philosophy debuted in the model T77, which melded Ledwinka's engineering and Jaray's aerodynamic research. Presented to the press in Berlin in March 1934, it was the first production car to take advantage of effective streamlining. Powered by either a 2.97 or 3.4 litre magnesium alloy, air-cooled V8 engine with a central camshaft and squirrel-cage cooling blowers, the six-passenger T77 limousine was capable of just over 90 mph. As early as 1935, a centrally-mounted third driving lamp became integral to the body design. Unfortunately, coach-built construction combined with its advanced technology resulted in the rear-engine, aero-dynamic Tatra 77 being quite expensive.

Continued development of the rear-engine, streamliner concept culminated in Tatra's model T87, which debuted in 1936 as a more affordable and simplified version of the T77. Styled along the same lines as its predecessor, it featured a sportier and more delicate shape than that of the stately and imposing T77. The newer car rode on a shorter wheelbase, and featured full monocoque construction in which the body and boxed central chassis became a strong and extremely safe single unit. Still mounted in the fork of the frame behind the passenger compartment, a more compact, 2.97 liter V8 still featured the magnesium alloy construction and blower cooling of the T77's, but employed a single camshaft per bank and hemispherical combustion chambers. Rubber mountings between the drive-train and body isolated the car's occupants from road noise and vibrations.

Simplified body construction and drivetrain engineering resulted in an overall weight reduction of 24 percent (946 pounds). Despite having only 75 hp, its lower weight and scientifically determined shape (with a drag coefficient of 0.36) allowed the T87 to reach a speed of approximately 100 mph — making it one of the fastest passenger sedans of its day. And, as a car capable of cruising steadily at speeds of 70 to 80 mph, it was clearly suited for the fine new roads appearing across Europe, while the independent suspension made it equally capable on the rough roads of its native land. However, the heavy rear-weight bias (62 percent) still saw a dangerous oversteer in the hands of unskilled drivers. Despite being more affordable than the T77, the T87 was still a luxurious and expensive automobile with highly advanced features and fine attention to detail.

Production of the T87 survived the Nazi regime's annexation of the Sudetenland in 1938, and except for 1943 and 1944, continued until 1950, at which time Czechoslovakia's new communist regime forced Tatra to stop work on all passenger cars and focus strictly on truck designs. The post-WWII Soviet occupation also found Tatra's visionary engineer imprisoned for alleged Nazi collaboration. When his six-year imprisonment ended in 1951, Ledwinka returned to his native Austria and left his greatest achievement — the Tatra T87— behind him.

Of the 3,000 T87s built, none were sold new in North America. For his second T87, Gary Cullen went to Czechoslovakia. Reported to have been owned by an influential member of the Czech Communist Party from Brno, Cullen found it at a restoration shop run by former Tatra workers in Koprivnice. The mechanical and structural work had been completed to an exacting standard and the car was ideally suited for extensive touring. He has since proven the soundness of Ledwinka and Jaray's 70-year-old design.

— JAS

Streamlined Eight-cylinder Passengers Car *Tatra 87* with air cooled • Rear—engine 160 km/H.

TAT R

A 8 7

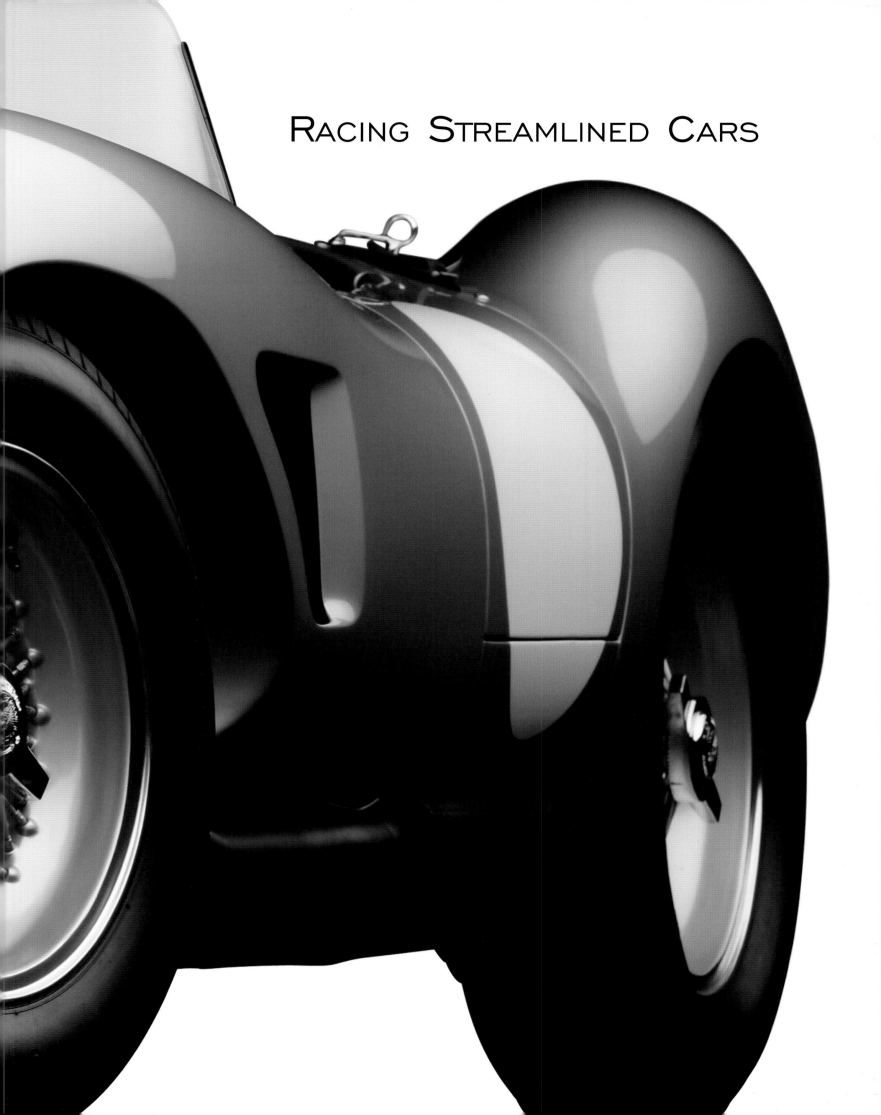

RACING STREAMLINED CARS

STREAMLINED FOR SPEED

In the early 20th century, racers understood that for *any* car to go faster, it needed a powerful engine, in the lightest possible chassis. The advent of streamlining followed more slowly. Consider pioneer aircraft. They were flimsy affairs with doped canvas and wire construction. But change was afoot.

It's unclear who initiated Barney Oldfield's radical Golden Submarine, designed by Harry Miller, but its appearance in 1917 surely started constructors thinking about cheating the wind. Most racecars of that period were double-wide to carry a riding mechanic. Few builders saw merit in vee-ed grilles, so the sole concession to streamlining might be an extended, pointed tail. The egg-shaped Golden Submarine, with its low, fully-enclosed cockpit, changed the picture briefly, but after a crash, Oldfield had the car rebuilt to resemble more contemporary, open-cockpit racers.

By the 1920's, the blazing, 140+ mph speeds of Board Track racers encouraged the construction of slender, elegant projectiles with narrow cockpits and tall thin tires that resembled the discs of a harrow. In 1924, on California's Muroc Dry Lake, Tommy Milton's 3-liter Miller 183 nearly set a world's speed record. Barely wider than Milton's shoulders, the car's slim cockpit and tapered tail, set racecar design standards for decades to follow.

Miller improved on that equation with his 122 front-drive car. Its narrow, low-mounted transaxle permitted a 9-inch lower seating position. The later, and even slimmer, Miller 91 FWD's coefficient of drag is unknown, but compared to taller rear-drive cars, it resembled a needle on wheels.

In 1927, Frank Lockhart's Land Speed Record V-16-engined (actually two 91-cid Miller Straight 8's on a common crankcase) Stutz Blackhawk was originally conceived with a fully-enveloped body, but designer Zenas Weisel, demurred, insisting the wheels be sheathed separately, the axles covered with fairings, and finned intercoolers be a portion of the hood. The result, built by Myron Stevens and Floyd Dreyer, was stunning, arguably the best representation of streamlining theory to date, and unsurpassed until the late '30s Mercedes-Benz and Auto-Union streamliners. Sadly, unbalanced forces from a blown tire at over 200-mph ended Lockhart's brief life and destroyed the Blackhawk.

Overseas, Voisin and Bugatti experimented with "tank" cars, perhaps so-called because their bodies resembled those of WWI tanks. Most racers resisted enclosed bodywork, and aerodynamic efforts were confined to minute but curvaceous grille and body refinements. The immensely powerful late-1930s Mercedes-Benz and Auto-Union Grand Prix racers, considered the most

Above: Barney Oldfield.
Opposite top: Oldfield with the Miller "Golden Submarine".
Opposite botom: Frank Lockhart in the Stutz Blackhawk at Daytona Beach, 1928.

advanced of their era were generally fitted with open wheel bodywork. However, the land speed record versions of both German racers featured fully-enveloping bodies.

Meanwhile, amateur racers, with scarce credentials, began experimenting as only people can do when they don't know what they don't know.

In 1940, an enterprising California hot rodder (and carpenter by profession), Bob Rufi, built a diminutive, cigar-shaped lakester, powered by a modified Chevrolet four-cylinder engine. So-Cal Speed Shop founder, Alex Xydias, was very impressed with Rufi's "intelligence, innovation and craftsmanship." The first hot rodder to successfully employ aerodynamics, Rufi's homebuilt car turned over 140 mph at Harper Dry Lake, a record that stood for ten years.

After WW II, British land speed record-seekers like John Cobb, George E.T. Eyston and Malcolm Campbell, built huge and very expensive aircraft-engined behemoths to break the 350-to-400 mph land speed barriers. Their sponsored efforts were impressive, but American ingenuity soon came to play.

Using mechanical and aircraft experience gained in the service, California hot rodders like ex-PT boat Navy vet, Bill Burke, devised simpler, cheaper high-speed solutions. After admiring a shapely 165-gallon drop tank for a P-51 Mustang on Guadalcanal, Burke intuitively knew the surplus bargain would make the perfect aerodynamic shape for a front-engined lakes racer. Built right after the war, the resulting "belly tanker" was too small, and the driver sat high.

Burke then reasoned he could get the driver down out of the airstream, and the engine in the rear, by modifying larger 315-gallon tanks, like

those originally fitted in pairs, so a twin-boom P-38 Lightning's thirsty Allison V-12's could carry fuel for lengthy combat patrols. In 1949, Burke's "Suite Sixteen" topped 150 mph and begat a series of fast "Belly Tank" racers, culminating in Alex Xydias' 198-mph Bonneville record in the So-Cal tank.

Bravery was second nature to these men. "The driver was not protected by a crush zone," Xydias later modestly told author, Mark Christensen "He *was* the crush zone. I'd never raced anything before, so I didn't know any better."

Stuart Hilborn, who invented modern fuel injection, was another enterprising hot rodder who built a sleek 150-mph lakester, with a body so narrow he had to wriggle into the cockpit by turning sideways. Other post-WWII rodders used sleek, track-car noses, tonneau covers and full belly pans to streamline their Model T, A, and Deuce roadsters. Bob Pierson, who'd worked at Douglas Aircraft, chopped his '34 Ford to record lows, then fabricated a tail-pan diffuser to ensure his record-setting coupe slipped through the air.

In the earliest days, a few makes had flirted with the rudiments of streamlining. As aircraft design became more sophisticated, the learning curve reversed itself and streamlining evolved from the efforts in the air, to influence automobiles on the ground. Working with Dean Batchelor, Alex Xydias made a major breakthrough.

Batchelor had read about the prewar streamlining efforts of Auto-Union and Mercedes-Benz. An ex-Army Air Corps B-17 crewman, he understood a fact that seemed counter-intuitive to many hot rodders: Doubling a car's frontal area, with the right-shaped body, could halve its coefficient of drag. Although neither man had ever taken on a project of this magnitude, Xydias and Batchelor, with several talented friends, built a fully-enclosed, experimental streamliner.

"We were influenced by Major Goldie Gardner's MG Special," Batchelor admits, but lacking serious sponsorship, except for an Edelbrock-equipped Ford flathead, the team did its best with what it could make from surplus parts and materials.

In 1949, at Bonneville, Batchelor was running at an astonishing 193-mph in the So-Cal Streamliner when both front tires shred their treads, injuring him, but thankfully not fatally, ending their first bold attempts, but evidencing great potential. Undaunted, and back again in 1950, the So-Cal team averaged 208-mph, breaking a long-standing 1928 American record held by Ray Keech. Next, they headed for Daytona Beach where, running at sea level, their engine would thus produce more power, and they could break the 219-mph International Class C record.

The Streamliner crashed again, but their baton, bravely carried, was taken up by others. Not long afterward, the "City of Burbank Streamliner"

broke the International Class C record with a 238-mph run. Incredulous Europeans found it hard to believe that their sophisticated, well-financed efforts had been stymied by "amateur" teams of talented hot rodders, who understood streamlining fundamentals and applied them to win, time after time.

Today, the restored So-Cal belly tank, owned by Bruce Meyer and on display here, epitomizes the cleverness and ingenuity of young men who overcame a lack of sophisticated knowledge with ingenuity and bold action.

Throughout the latter half of the 20th century, benefiting from advances in wind tunnel experimentation, computer modeling, and ultimately from advanced aircraft practice, automotive stylists have adapted nearly every nuance — from tailfins and wings, to spoilers and NACA ducts — initially in racecars, then expressed in contemporary auto design.

– KG

1937 DELAHAYE 145 "MILLION FRANC PRIZE"

The Delahaye Company was noted for creating extraordinary streamlined road and racing cars, but in 1937, when it decided to participate in the Million Franc Prize race, it took a different path with a radically different design. Its Delahaye 145 racecar (chassis 48771) was strictly utilitarian. Its metal alloy coachwork tightly sheathed the chassis and snub-nosed grille with no frills or flourishes. Its engineers never tested the car in a wind tunnel, relying instead on their experience and intuition and the power of the car's unsupercharged 4.5 liter V-12 engine and the aerodynamic properties of its low-slung and well-balanced chassis.

The Million Franc Race prize was to be awarded to the first car to break the record set in 1934 by Louis Chiron driving the Alfa Romeo at Montlhéry at an average speed of 146.508 km/hr over 200 km. The record had to be broken by midnight of August 31, 1937. On August 27, four days before the deadline, driver René Dreyfus put in the performance of a lifetime and his Delahaye 145 set a new record with an average speed of 146.654 km/hr over 200 km. France went wild.

By the beginning of July, Delahaye engineer Jean François and Dreyfus were at the Montlhéry

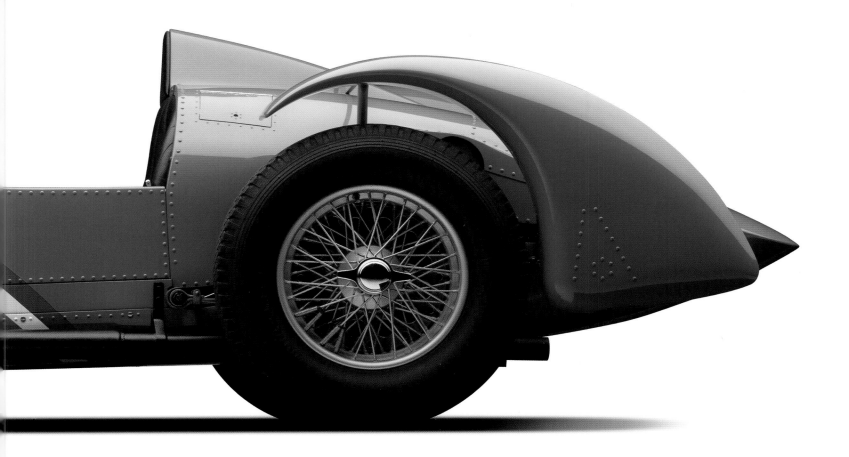

racetrack almost daily. The necessary speed had to top the old record for sixteen laps or 200 kilometers, from a standing start. To achieve the average, the driver had to make very careful calculations.

In an unpublished interview by Jean-Paul Caron in 1973, René Dreyfus explained that the car was lightened as much as possible. "We kept tinkering, changing things here and there; we worked on the brakes, we worked on everything to try to increase the power. At one point I had a rather stern discussion with Jean François and told him that I couldn't go through the Ascari bend at more than a given speed. He didn't agree with me, and so I told him, 'It's very simple, take the

car, get in, take my goggles, and you'll see.' So he got into the car, took my goggles, left, and after two or three laps, he stopped, saying he was very sorry but that he couldn't reach that speed, that it wasn't possible on the Ascari bend." Every effort was made to lighten each piece of the car and it was continually returned to the factory to improve its performance. Finally, the number 48771 was engraved on the top surface of the left frame rail.

The second contender for the prize was the Bugatti team, led by Jean Bugatti. Jean-Pierre Wimille was to have been the primary driver, but he was injured in a car accident on the way to the track. Although not as fast as his colleague,

Robert Benoist filled in for Wimille and began practicing immediately. On August 23, Jean Bugatti decided to make his attempt. Benoist did his best, but the press described his performance as "hesitant." He failed to qualify for the Million by nine-and-a-half seconds. The disappointed team was forced to pin its hopes upon a recovering Jean-Pierre Wimille.

In the meantime, René Dreyfus was also hard at work each day at Montlhéry, but he was unhappy with his speed on the crucial first lap. He kept telling Charles Weiffenbach (Monsieur Charles), general manager of Delahaye, that he wasn't ready for the final attempt. Monsieur Charles arrived on August 26, to convince his vacillating driver that he could win. Dreyfus was unmoved, claiming he needed more time to prepare. But Monsieur Charles had a trick up his sleeve and, when Dreyfus arrived at the track on August 27, he found that there would be no tests that day. Instead, in his words, "the whole press corps was at the track to watch my attempt to beat the record."

"To say that I was angry is an understatement," continued Dreyfus. "Normally I'm the gentlest man in the world. But Monsieur Charles had decided and the French press plus the foreign press were there, not to mention Jean François. The crowd had read about it in the morning papers, and would soon begin arriving." He was faced with a fait accompli.

Dreyfus was tense and refused to talk to anyone. The mechanics had worked all night on the car but at the scheduled 7 a.m. start time, it was still not ready. Finally, by 9 a.m., the Automobile Club called to ask if he was ready, and his response was to get into the car. According to Dreyfus, "I drove as I had never driven in my life." When he came in, he had broken the record at 1 hour 21 minutes 49 5/10 seconds, 146.654 km/hr. On Friday, August 27 he had won the Million— for the moment.

Later that same day, Wimille arrived by airplane from Nice, still not recovered completely but determined to win. There were rumors that the Bugatti would not compete, but Dreyfus had to be ready to take to the track immediately. "For four full days," he said, "we suffered. You had to consider, for instance, that a competitor might know he had more power than I had, and could attempt his performance at the last minute on August 31. This meant that I would have to start when dusk had fallen, which I preferred not to do. In any case, I was there constantly from morning till night." However, the day before the deadline, the Delahaye team spoke to the Automobile Club of France and was able to obtain permission to start two minutes after the Bugatti, should driver Wimille begin his try around dusk.

On Tuesday, August 31, Wimille finally started at 6:43 p.m. with Dreyfus following two minutes later. Dreyfus drove like a tiger, surpassing the speed he'd achieved when he broke the record on August 27. "I had decided," he said, "that if by chance Jean-Pierre broke down, I would stop, so that I could keep the record I'd set the week before, given the fact that it was not worth it at that hour to try and risk even more. Finally, at the end of seven or eight laps, I received the signal that I'd beaten the record of the week before. Then I found myself getting ahead of him in speed, although I had started later, and when I went past the pit, I saw Jean-Pierre's car stopped and some smoke around the pit. I think he'd had piston trouble. Nevertheless, suspecting that there still might be a little trick behind it all, I did not stop immediately. It was only two or three laps later that my wife and Monsieur Charles gave me the clear sign: "You did it, you have the record."

The exuberant crowd surged onto the field, and it was all over. Bugatti had abandoned the attempt. The Million belonged to Delahaye, to the Écurie Bleue team of Lucy Schell which had funded the effort and to René Dreyfus. "I came up to Jean-Pierre," remembered Dreyfus, "and I shook his hand. Wimille congratulated me. 'The best man won,' he said, and then added with a smile, 'My turn next!'"

After its famous victory, Chassis 48771 went on to race again. However, before it ran in the 1939 Mille Miglia, it was rebodied with a faired-in headrest and cycle fenders that were teardrop shaped and individually enclosed to reduce drag. Several years after the end of World War II, when it was no longer competitive, it was exhibited at a museum in France, although few recalled its glorious past. Fortunately, it was discovered by collector Jim Hull, who bought it with partner Peter Mullin. They both recognized its historical value, and sent it to England for restoration.

After three years of work, the car participated in the Mille Miglia Retrospective and was then sent to California. In 2006, the winner of the Million Franc Race won first prize in its class at the Pebble Beach Concours d'Elegance. It is now in the Peter Mullin Collection in Los Angeles.

– RA & DM

Following spread: At Montlhéry, René Dreyfus is ready for his record run to begin. He successfully averaged 146.654 km/hr over 200 km to earn the Million Franc Prize for Delahaye and Écurie Bleue. To the right of the car, Robert Benoist is flanked by a pair of mechanics.

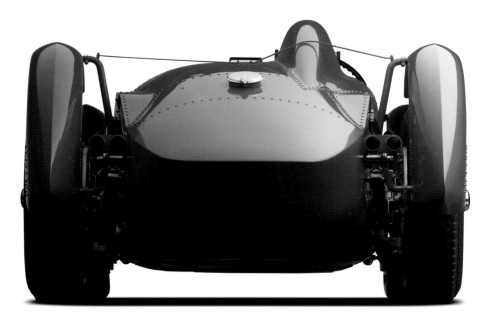

1952 So-Cal Belly Tanker

It was a form shaped to cut through the air at upwards of 275 mph with the least possible drag while carrying 2,000 pounds of fuel. Originally intended for service thousands of feet above the Pacific, the same shape worked effectively inches from the hard-packed surface of a California dry lake bed.

While in the South Pacific during World War II, a very sharp hot-rodder named Bill Burke spotted a 165 gallon detachable aluminum belly tank from P-51 and P-47 fighter aircraft. Burke figured that if the lightweight tank was strong enough to keep its shape while carrying more than 1,000

pounds of fuel and create very little drag in the air, it would work just as well on the dry lakes of California. These auxiliary tanks were suspended below the wings of aircraft to extend their range. If the planes came under fire, the pilot would jettison the tanks to reduce weight and drag. Otherwise, the tanks remained in place and were reused on subsequent missions.

Burke was the first hot rodder to make use of a surplus 165 gallon tank. It worked in theory, but the package was just too small to accommodate a V-8 engine, a driver and a rudimentary cooling system. The larger 315 gallon tanks from a P-38

proved even more suitable as they were big enough to accommodate a normal-sized driver in front of a large V-8 engine.

No belly tank dry lakes racer is better known than the So-Cal Special, originally campaigned by Dave DeLangton of Burbank, California. Eventually fitted with the very potent Ford V-8 60 engines of So-Cal Speed Shop owner Alex Xydias, the pair fielded a formidable competitor in the fierce stakes for pure speed that raged on the dry lakes of Southern California. Initial outings in June and July 1951 at El Mirage Dry Lake were inauspicious. However, during the Bonneville National Speed Trials held from August 27th to September 2nd, the team achieved real success when DeLangton drove the car to a

new A Class record 145.395 mph for the measured mile. With a larger 259 cid, Edelbrock-equipped Mercury engine, the car set a B Class record of 181.085. Another engine change to a 296 cid Mercury saw the So-Cal dry lakes racer reach 195.77 mph to land the C Class record.

Just as the original belly tanks were built for a specific purpose—so, too, were the "lakesters" built around those discarded tanks. Unlike many automobiles, because the So-Cal Special lakester was built to accommodate an existing shape, the body was not designed in the sense of most vehicles. The tank had sufficient width to accommodate a Ford or Mercury Flathead V-8, a broad-shouldered American driver and custom-fabricated chassis rails. However, suspension, brakes and wheels were positioned outboard of the body. Although most of the suspension components were pulled from existing cars, they were heavily drilled for lightness and to reduce wind resistance. Even the suspension arms and backing plates for the hydraulic brake drums and backing plates fitted to the Ford rear axle were drilled for lightness. By 1952, when the car achieved its greatest success, suspension was by torsion bars. However, the brakes and suspension were really secondary on such a car. Its whole purpose was to go fast in a straight line on an extremely smooth surface. After a run, the car had miles in which to slow and thus didn't require particularly powerful brakes—which is why none were fitted to the front wheels.

The So-Cal Special was by no means unique in using a surplus belly tank as its body. Many other lakesters started with a surplus fuel tank, a flathead Ford and Ford axles. What set it apart was the attention that went into its construction and race preparation. All the So-Cal cars, whether roadsters or lakesters, were always distinguished by their gleaming red and white paint and their exceptional appearance.

In many ways, a belly tank dry lakes car is a much purer expression of streamlining than most automobiles, simply because it was built for the uncompromised purpose of straight line speed. There was no consideration for driver comfort, engine cooling, bumpers or lighting. At the same time, the car was not very nimble and could hardly stop on a dime.

For 1953, the Lakester returned to competition, but by then the Flathead was no longer *the* engine to have. Powerful overhead-valve V-8s from GM and Chrysler had eclipsed the affordable and charismatic Ford. Eventually, the Lakester was sold sans engine. After many owners and a long and quiet sojourn in private hands, it was acquired by Southern California collector Bruce Meyer and sent to hot rod builder Pete Chapouris for a comprehensive restoration to its 1952 configuration, complete with a flathead engine built by Bob Meeks.

– JAS

Spread 166-167: The immaculately turned out So-Cal Belly Tank Lakester during the 1952 Bonneville National Speed Trials.

ALEX
XYDIAS

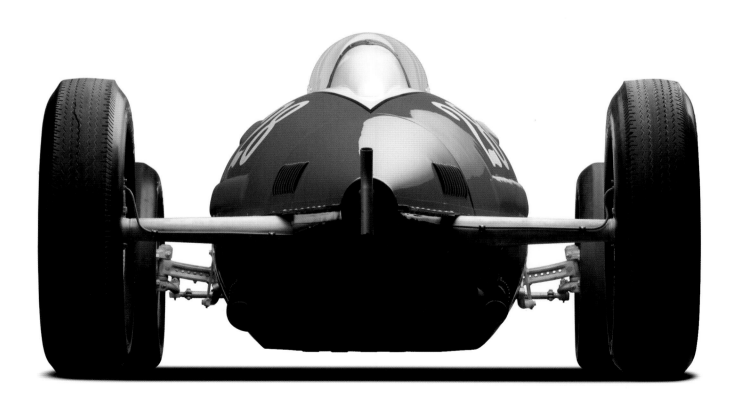

1957 FERRARI 625/250 TRC

Cognoscenti argue that Ferrari's most beautiful cars, both for racing and the road, were built in the mid-1950s. You only have to look at this 1957 625/250 TRC for proof. It is a stunning example, with a most interesting history.

Conceived in the rubble of a bombed-out factory in war-torn Modena, Italy, Ferrari was created by a bold, powerful man who had briefly been a racer himself, and who had later managed the prewar Alfa-Romeo Grand Prix team. Enzo Ferrari's young company entered competition immediately following its birth in 1947, and was soon selling high-performance cars in the United States.

The legendary Luigi Chinetti won the grueling 24 hours of Le Mans in a Ferrari 166MM Barchetta in June, 1949, for the marque's first major sports car victory. Two weeks later, he repeated that feat at the Spa 24 hours. When Enzo Ferrari questioned whether his fledgling company should risk its reputation so soon on another high-profile endurance race, Chinetti stood firm. "I said to Ferrari, 'We must show this was no accident.'" It wasn't. Chinetti won again.

After a brief period where Italy's finest *carrozzerias* vied for the honor of designing Ferrari coachwork, Pinin Farina (the name changed to Pininfarina in 1961) prevailed. Much of the actual construction

was done at Sergio Scaglietti's shop in Modena. Scaglietti was also responsible for many of the Ferrari competition car designs. Italian marque historian, Winston Goodfellow wrote, "Ferrari would often send Scaglietti a rolling chassis saying, 'Make this one a roadster, that one a coupe.' It was then up to Scaglietti to create what he thought best."

Italy's Emilia-Romagna province—where Scaglietti and many other coachbuilders were located—was renowned for its armorers during the Middle Ages. Many of their metal fabricating techniques evolved into coach craft practices of the highest order. Scaglietti's shop would first form the outline of a body with thin metal tubing, fashioning a wire framework called a marquette. After the essential design was created, lightweight panels were formed by meticulously hammering thin sheets of

aluminum over sandbags and well-worn tree stumps, until the desired shape was achieved.

Enduring Scaglietti designs like the legendary Testa Rossa and the 250 GTO Berlinetta evolved from, what seems today, a deceptively simple process. Scaglietti himself had no formal design training. Goodfellow, who has interviewed Scaglietti extensively, reports that Sergio designed cars, in his own words, "by the eyes alone, not making even the most rudimentary of sketches."

Competition Ferraris were not just successful. Thanks to Sergio Scaglietti, they were simply beautiful. Luigi Chianti's pioneering efforts in America ensured Ferrari was well-represented. John Von Neumann was the perfect Ferrari dealer for Los Angeles. Comfortable with Hollywood

SERGIO SCAGLIETTI

glitterati, he actively raced his cars, and his stature allowed him to request special models from the factory that he was sure would appeal to a wealthy clientele, such as the graceful, open-topped, 250 California Spyder.

Von Neumann owned a 250 Testa Rossa (the name, which means "red head" in Italian, referred to selected Ferrari high-performance cylinder heads, which were painted in a red crackle finish), and raced it successfully, but preferred the more nimble handling of the lighter four-cylinder 625 TRC. Von Neuman had a pair of TRCs, 0672 and 0680. Both of the Von Neumann cars were essentially 500 TRCs that had been upgraded with the 625 (2.5-liter) version of Ferrari's DOHC four-cylinder engine.

Von Neumann had Richie Ginther and Paul Primeau install a 300-bhp, twin-cam, six-carbure-tor, 3-liter, 250 TR V-12 in 0672 MDTR (Mondial Testa Rossa) creating, in essence, a Ferrari hot rod. The resulting 625/250 TRC was raced by Von Neumann until 1959, then sold to Otto Zipper. After a few more active seasons, where it was driven by the legendary Ken Miles, the 625/250 TRC passed through various hands, was fitted, at one point, with a Ford V-8 engine for drag racing, then disappeared.

Beverly Hills collector (and former Von Neumann Porsche customer) Bruce Meyer was fascinated by the notion of a Ferrari factory hot rod and he began a search for the Von Neumann 625/250 TRC. His quest was intensified when he realized only one of these cars had been built, but he was stymied when knowledgeable Ferrari brokers insisted the car could not be found.

Undaunted, Meyer discovered that the Von Neumann 625/250 TRC had been sold by Christie's in Monaco in 1991, then went to a Dutchman named Charles Zwolsman. He was involved in a drug bust in Holland in 1993, and the Ferrari was impounded by the Dutch government.

When, at last, this long sought-after Ferrari was offered in a sealed-bid government auction, Bruce Meyer was the winning bidder. Reunited with the 3-liter V-12 that Von Neumann had installed, it received a meticulous restoration by Richard Freshman, Phil Reilly and Steve Beckman.

"For me, this Ferrari is a dream come true," says Meyer. "Its great looks, the sound of its V-12 engine, and its fascinating history, make it an intoxicating package. I love to drive this car; I drove it to Pasadena for the photo shoot for this exhibit."

While the 625/250 TRC lacks the distinctive cutaways of the classic early Testa Rossas, whose dramatically-flared front wheel openings remain that model's design signature, it's arguably more aerodynamic.

And it bears repeating that this Ferrari, and many like it from the atelier of the prolific Sergio Scaglietti, never benefited from a single wind-tunnel study. Scaglietti told Winston Goodfellow that he understood "the more aerodynamic a car was, the more beautiful it became."

With its enclosed headlights, long hood, cozy cockpit, short deck, driver's faired headrest, and dramatically low windscreen, the 625/250 TRC remains a shining example of the pre-CAD (computer-assisted design) era, where the discerning eye and skilled hands of an acknowledged Italian artisan was all it took to create a rolling masterpiece.

The story of the evolution of Ferrari TRC 0672 is very much the history of Southern California sports car racing in microcosm — "When you're no longer competitive, drop in a bigger mill." So, whatever Italian Ferrari purists may say about Meyer's stunning 625/250, the Von Neumann's respectable placings and Ginther's victory at Lago de Guadalupe, Mexico, in this car are proof that it is very real and very California.

–KG

Opposite: Ferrari distributor and dealer Von Neumann (top) favored the handling of the TRC over that of the bigger 250 Testa Rossa. His solution was to have a 250 V-12 inserted into the TRC engine bay. Much of the engine conversion work was performed by Ken Miles (bottom) who achieved some excellent results in the TRC.

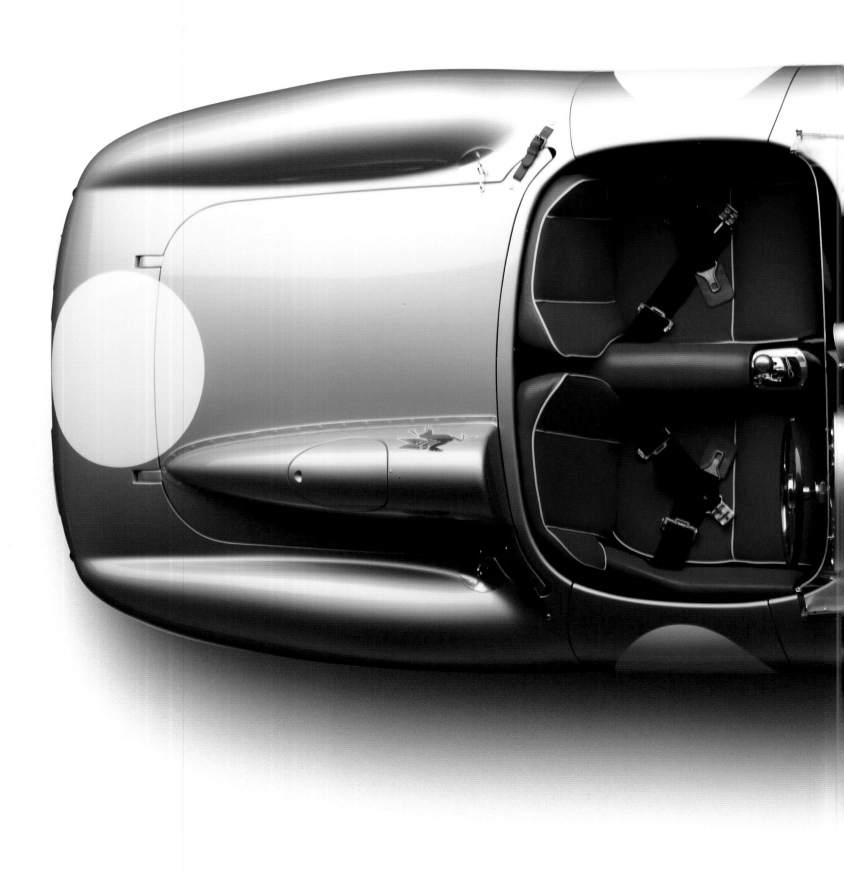

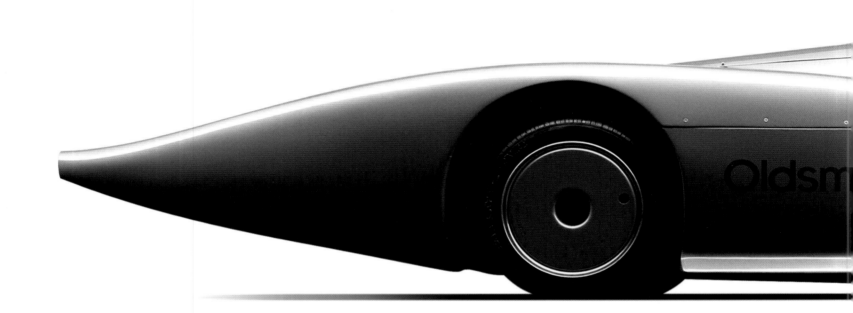

1987 OLDSMOBILE AEROTECH

It looked like a cross between a German speed record car of the 1930s and a modern endurance-racing prototype. In fact, it was unlike any Oldsmobile that ever existed — before or since. But the Oldsmobile Aerotech is an appropriate bookend in Oldsmobile history; its record speed accomplishments are a fitting contrast to the 1901 Curved Dash Olds, the world's first mass-produced car.

On August 27, 1989, under big skies amid the high desert scrubland at the Fort Stockton Test Center at Fort Stockton, Texas, racing's immortal A.J. Foyt put the Aerotech to the test. In so doing, he estab-

lished a closed-course speed record of 257.123 mph in a short-tailed version, the ST, to break a previous record of 250.918 mph set in 1979 by a twin-turbocharged V-8 Mercedes-Benz. Foyt also set a new flying mile speed record of 267.399 mph with a long-tailed version, the LT, to break the previous record of 254.578 mph set in 1959 at the Bonneville Salt Flats by a supercharged MG.

Amazingly, the feat was accomplished with a 2.3-liter DOHC four-cylinder powerplant — the Quad 4, equipped with turbos to boost power output to 1,000 hp.

The Aerotech was an aberration from a company that specialized in cushy, conservative American transportation. But in the late 1980s, Olds was keen to drum up visibility and support for one of GM's first high-volume DOHC engines. The twin cam Quad 4 was destined to power Olds Calais mid-sized cars as well as Pontiac Grand Ams. The Aerotech project appeared to be the perfect vehicle to promote the prowess of the 16-valve four-cylinder.

"The Aerotech car was designed specifically to prove the high performance capabilities of the Quad 4 engine," said Oldsmobile chief engineer Ted Louckes in a 1989 press release celebrating the achievement. "We wanted to extend engine

technology to the outer limits and to demonstrate the capability of this engine in an extreme testing environment."

Louckes noted that the Oldsmobile Aerotech engine maintains the general configuration of the production engine, but with a specially-developed turbocharger. The short-tailed version was equipped with a single turbo while the long-tailed version was fitted with twin turbochargers.

The Aerotech was built on a modified March Indy-car chassis, while Goodyear contributed a special version of its Eagle GT racing tire developed for ultra-high speeds. With its carbon fiber body, the Aerotech weighed only 1,600 pounds

ED
WELBURN

and stood a mere 40 inches high. Its width was 86 inches, with a wheelbase of 111.3 inches and a length of 192 inches. As a high-speed record chaser, the car was designed to travel at high speeds with a ground clearance of less than an inch.

The architect for the Aerotech was none other than Ed Welburn, who would later ascend to the top position in GM's global design organization, becoming only the sixth design leader in GM history. Welburn says he was inspired by the cars that run at Le Mans, especially the long-tailed Porsche 917s.

Chuck Jordan, then head of GM Design, knew about Welburn's passion for racing cars and offered him a chance to design the Aerotech. "The first sketch I did was taken to Chuck Jordan and he said, 'That's it,' says Welburn. "The first sketch became the car. The engineers and tire guys adjusted it a bit, but the actual theme remained the same."

I wanted a design that went beyond a regular race car," adds Welburn. "It needed to be a well-developed sculpted shape. Very few race cars have that form of execution from end to end."

The original design was the short-tailed version, which is what Oldsmobile wanted, but Welburn was convinced that the long tail was better for aero on straight-line runs by letting the air continue to flow along the body until it is released at a narrow point at the rear of the car, thus minimizing drag.

Creating sufficient down force with low drag drove the design. The goal was a drag number that was less than half of an Indy car. Welburn worked in the wind tunnel with engineer Max Schenkel, who is still with GM today.

"We spent days in the wind tunnel working with a clay one-third scale model. During the day I was designing a Cutlass Supreme and, at night, I was in the wind tunnel with Max and the Aerotech."

The finished long tail bears some resemblance to the Auto Union and Mercedes speed record cars that Hitler used to promote the engineering prowess of the Third Reich in the late 1930s. But there were differences as well, including an underbody on the Aerotech that featured a large tunnel to create a low pressure area as air passed through, thus providing down force.

Welburn's design includes the capability of adjusting underbody sections to control the distribution of down force front to rear. The shape of the body also allows for self-aligning torque when the vehicle is in yaw.

GM built a total of three Aerotechs — two short tails and one long tail. "What I'm most proud of is that there are no wings or spoilers or other tack-on devices (except for the rear wing on the short-tailed car)," says Welburn.

Five years after setting the record at Fort Stockton, the Aerotech came back again in December 1992 with a different powerplant, the Aurora V-8, and set another 47 FIA speed records at Fort Stockton. These included 10,000 and 25,000 kilometer world speed-endurance records, formerly held by Mercedes-Benz, as well as international and American records ranging from the 10 kilometer speed-endurance record to the 24-hour speed records. These records were accomplished by a dedicated team of Oldsmobile drivers piloting the Aerotech 24 hours a day for eight days.

Although their record duties — and Oldsmobile itself — are of the past, General Motors has retained the three Aerotechs, which are housed at the GM Heritage Center in suburban Detroit, along with many other historical GM vehicles. They can take their places right next to the 1901 Curved Dash Olds as automotive gemstones.

– JM

Top: The fluid lines of the Oldsmobile Aerotech are broken only by a single front NACA duct and a pair of inlets for the side mounted radiators.

Bottom: A GM modeler works on the detailing of a scale model of the Aerotech.

Following spread: GM tapped race driver A.J. Foyt to drive the Aerotech. Foyt set a new record of 257.123 mph at the Fort Stockton track in Texas.

1994 McLaren F1

As racers, their passion was to create the ultimate road car. And they did — with a vengeance. The McLaren F1 is perhaps the best example in automotive history of a no-compromise road machine.

This car was the offspring of a Formula One racing brain trust, which conceived the idea one day in 1988 while waiting for a delayed flight at Milan's Linate Airport. The group consisted of McLaren CEO Ron Dennis, engineer Gordon Murray, marketer Creighton Brown and share-holder Mansour Ojjeh.

What makes the McLaren F1 and its siblings so remarkable are their extremes of high power, low weight, and advanced aerodynamics. It boasts a litany of technological firsts, including the first truly carbon-fiber monocoque structure for a road car, a fully active fan-assisted ground-effect system and a central driving position with two slightly rearward passenger seats.

Power came from a purpose-built BMW all-aluminum 48-valve 6.0 liter V-12 providing 627 hp in road car specification. The McLaren is also one of the lightest supercars ever built at 2,509

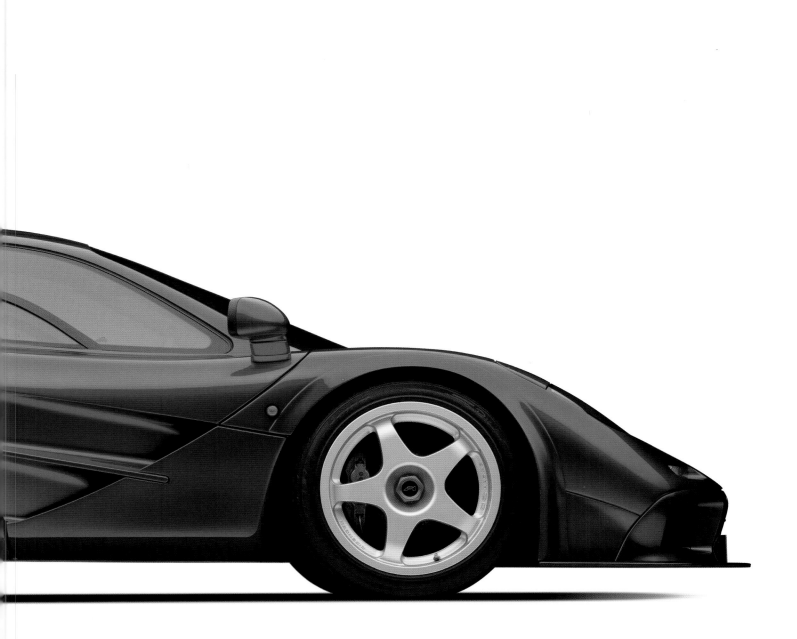

pounds, which enabled a race car-like power-to-weight ratio. The F1 established a record top speed for a production car, attaining 240.1 mph at a speed run at Volkswagen's Ehra Leissen test track near Wolfsburg Germany on March 31, 1998. Despite the car being more than 10 years old, its record speed has since been exceeded by only two cars — the 1000 hp Bugatti Veyron and the 806 hp Swedish Konigsegg CCR, both in 2005.

Gordon Murray moved from his position as design director of the McLaren Formula One team and set out to produce a road car with excellent handling characteristics and proper downforce — "without adding mass to the car to be accelerated, braked and resisted in cornering," according to Doug Nye in his excellent McLaren

F1 documentary book, *Driving Ambition*. Aided by stylist Peter Stevens, formerly of Lotus, who penned the latest iteration of the Lotus Espirit and the second-generation Lotus Elan before moving to McLaren, the F1 was designed to make full use of ground-effect technology.

The car features a fan-assisted full underbody air management system, but the fans don't generate downforce in the same manner as the Brabham Formula One "fan car," or the Chaparral 2J "sucker car."

The underbody features a diffuser at the rear, which is divided into three sections — a central diverging section, with two small reflex diffusers at each side. The diverging section works in the normal way by

GORDON
MURRAY

decelerating the air from under the car, thus creating a low-pressure area under the floor-pan. The reflex diffusers require the boundary layer to be drawn off, and this is where the fans enter the equation.

The fans are relatively small and draw air from the front of the two side diffusers to remove the boundary layer. In typical McLaren fashion, this air is then used to cool the ECUs before being blown into the engine compartment to cool the engine ancilliaries.

The ultimate road car proved to be something that racers couldn't resist. The McLaren F1 was so good that it not only won its inaugural race at Le Mans — in special F1 GTR trim — in 1995, but also finished third, fourth and fifth and 13th in the same race. To commemorate the occasion, McLaren built five LM models, which were thinly disguised race cars with 680 hp engines and rear wings.

The McLaren shown here is chassis number 11, which was originally built in 1994. It was returned to McLaren between 1999 and 2001 for conversion to a High Downforce Configuration which, in addition to the air management system under the car, features a rear wing based on the 1995 Le Mans car. This provides significant downforce, which is reacted by a much stiffer suspension. With this aerodynamic change, there was a significant improvement in cornering and road holding.

To balance the downforce at the rear, the front bodywork is modified with a front splitter and small diffusers in front of each rear wheel. The result is a car with very high cornering capability.

Other changes made by McLaren to this car include the 18-inch road wheel option, satellite navigation (including remote control), up-rated air conditioning, intercom system and three pairs of headsets, 14-inch steering wheel, gas discharge headlights, passenger over-carpets and tinted side windows. These modifications are typical of the work McLaren does to meet each owner's specific requirements.

All told, the F1 was built in three different body styles. The original F1 was built without wings or body appendages and a total of 64 cars were constructed. Far more exclusive were the five F1 LMs built to commemorate the 1995 Le Mans victory. Rarer still is the F1 GT built to homologate the 1997 GTR race cars, of which only three were built. Rounding out the remaining production of 100 cars were 28 F1 GTR racers built between 1995 and 1997. The very last of 107 total cars (including prototypes) was completed on May 25, 1998.

McLaren maintains utmost confidentiality regarding who owns these prestigious machines, with any public knowledge being at the discretion of the owner. Suffice it to say that some of the most notable automotive collectors in the world have a McLaren F1 in their stable. Currently with its third owner, chassis number 11 is part of the private Cavallino Holdings Collection, which acquired it in 2003.

While the original cars sold for over a million dollars a copy in the mid 1990s, their value today is significantly higher.

— JM

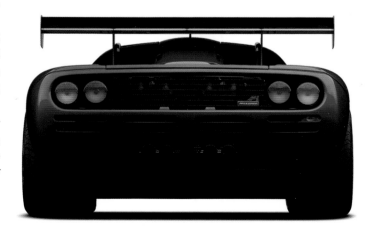

SUGGESTED READING/SOURCES

Adatto, Richard and Meredith, Diana; *Delahaye Styling and Design*; Dalton Watson Fine Books; Deerfield, IL, 2006.

Adatto, Richard; *From Passion To Perfection: The Story of French Streamlined Styling*; Editions SPE Barthélémy; Paris, 2003.

Adatto, Richard and Meredith, Diana; *Delage Styling and Design*; Dalton Watson Fine Books; Deerfield, IL, 2005.

Armi, C. Edson; *The Art of American Automobile Design*; Pennsylvania University Press, University Park, 1988.

Armi, C. Edson; *American Car Design Now: Inside the Studios of America's Top Car Designers*; UCSB, Santa Barbara, 2004.

Banham, Reyner; *Design By Choice*; Rizzoli; New York, 1981

Batchelor, Dean; "*Fuel For Thought: The So-Cal Speed Shop Special;*" Automobile Quarterly; Volume 34; Number 1, October 1995.

Borgeson, Griffith; *Errett Loban Cord*; Automobile Quarterly, Princeton, 1983.

Bush, Donald J.: *The Streamlined Decade*; George Braziller, Inc., New York, 1975.

Conway, Hugh; *Bugatti: Le Pur-Sang des Automobiles*; Haynes Publishing Company; Sparkford, UK, 1987.

Damman, George H; *70 Years of Chrysler* (revised edition); Crestline Publishing; Sarasota, FL, 1974.

Damman, George H. and Wagner, James K.; *The Cars of Lincoln Mercury*; Crestline Publishing; Sarasota, FL, 1987.

De Dubé, B.P.D; "The Constant Czech;" *Automobile Quarterly*; Volume 7; Number 3, Winter 1969.

Dominguez, Henry; *Edsel Ford and E. T. Gregorie*; SAE International; Warrendale, PA, 1999.

Dreyfus, René and Kimes, Beverly Rae; *My Two Lives*; Aztek; Tucson, AZ, 1983.

Ellman-Brown, Michael; *Bentley: The Silent Sports Car 1931-1941*; Dalton Watson, London, 1989.

Egan, Phillip S.; *Design and Destiny: The Making of the Tucker Automobile*; On the Mark Publications; Orange, CA, 1989.

Egan, Phillip S.; "*Tremulis: The Genius Behind the Tucker;*" Automobile Quarterly; Vol. 26, No. 3, Third Quarter 1988.

Furman, Michael; *Motor Cars of the Classic Era*; Coachbuilt Press; New York, 2003.

Gelernter, David; *1939: The Lost World of the Fair*; Random House; New York, 1995.

Georgano, Nick; *The Beaulieu Encyclopedia of the Automobile*; The Stationery Office; London, 2000.

Georgano, Nick; *The Beaulieu Encyclopedia of the Automobile: Coachbuilding*; The Stationery Office; London, 2001.

Hanks, David A. and Hoy, Anne; *American Streamlined Design: The World of Tomorrow*; Flammarion; Paris, 2005.

Kimes, Beverly Rae, *The Classic Era,* Classic Car Club of America, Des Plaines, Illinois, 2001.

Kimes, Beverly Rae; *The Standard Catalog of American Cars*: 1805-1942; Krause Publications; Iola, Wisconsin; 1985.

LaMarre, Thomas S.; "*Stout's Scarab: A Challenge and a Prophesy;*" Automobile Quarterly; Vol. 29, No. 4, August 1991.

Lamm, Michael and Holls, David; *A Century of Automotive Style;* Lamm-Morada Publishing; Stockton, CA, 1996.

Lichtenstein, Claude and Engler, Franz; *Streamlined: A Metaphor for Progress: The Esthetics of Minimized Drag*, Lars Müller Publishers, Baden, Switzerland; 1996.

Lynch, Michael; "*TRC Hot Rod;*" Cavallino; No. 152, April/May 2006

Moore, Simon; *The Immortal 2.9: Alfa Romeo 8C-2900 A & B*; Parkside; Seattle, 1986.

MacMin, Strother and Lamm, Michael; *Detroit Style: Automotive Form, 1925-1950*. Detroit Institute of Arts; Detroit,1985.

Meikle, Jeffrey; *Twentieth Century Limited: Industrial Design in America*, 1925-1939; Temple University Press; Philadelphia, 1979.

Museum of Contemporary Art in Los Angeles; *Automobile and Culture*; Harry Abrams; New York, 1984.

Nye, Doug; *Driving Ambition: The Official Inside Story of the McLaren F1*; McLaren Cars; Woking, UK, 1999.

Rosenbusch, Karla A.; "*In the Eye of the Beholder: Chrysler Airflow;*" Automobile Quarterly Vol. 38, No. 3, December 1998.

Sloniger, Jerry; "*The Slippery Shapes of Paul Jaray;*" Automobile Quarterly; Vol. 13, No. 3, Third Quarter 1975.

Stein, Jonathan A. ; "*Milanese Masterpiece; Alfa Romeo 8C-2900B By Touring;*" Automobile Quarterly; Vol. 37, No. 1, October 1997.

Tremulis, Alex; "*Created by the Measured Mile;*" Special-Interest Autos; Number 28, May/June 1975.

Wilson, Richard Guy and Pilgrim, Diane H.; *The Machine Age in America: 1918-1941* Harry N. Abrams; New York, 1986.

CONTRIBUTOR BIOGRAPHIES

An authority on French aerodynamic cars produced before World War II, **Richard Adatto** sits on the Advisory Board of the Pebble Beach Concours d'Elegance and has judged at Pebble Beach and Meadow Brook Hall for more than 20 years. The French car technical advisor for the Classic Car Club of America, Adatto has written several books, a variety of magazine articles and scripts for automotive TV programs. He resides in Seattle, Washington.

Terry Boyce began writing a car column for his hometown newspaper at age 18. After gaining experience at *Special-Interest Autos* under Mike Lamm, he joined the *Old Cars Weekly* staff, becoming editor in 1977. He has authored several books and many magazine articles on automotive subjects. He worked on Chevrolet marketing communications at Campbell-Ewald for more than 20 years, retiring from the agency in 2006. Recently, he became Director of Operations for the Meadow Brook Concours d'Elegance.

David Burgess-Wise has been writing about antique automobiles since the early 1960s and has published some 30 books and hundreds of articles on the subject. Keenly interested in coachbuilding, he is Honorary Archivist of the Worshipful Company of Coachmakers and Coach Harness Makers of London. He also sits on the Advisory Council of Britain's National Motor Museum and is a consultant to Bonhams auctioneers. His small collection of includes a 1926 Delage DISS and a 1903 De Dion-Bouton.

Michael Furman first picked up a camera as a young boy to photograph a 1963 Corvette Split Window Coupe. Throughout his 33-year career he has specialized in studio lighting of classic cars: from Bugatti and Bentley, to Duesenberg, Delahaye and Alfa Romeo. Furman's work can regularly be seen in other Coachbuilt Press publications as well as in automotive magazines from Europe, America and Asia.

Ken Gross has been an automotive writer for 35 years. His credits include *Playboy*, *Hemispheres*, The *Rodder's Journal* and edmunds.com. He wrote the acclaimed TV Series, "Behind the Headlights." Formerly Director of the Petersen Automobile Museum in Los Angeles, Gross has been a Pebble Beach Judge for 18 years and is the chief Class Judge for the Historic Hot Rod Class. He lives in Hamilton, Virginia.

Beverly Rae Kimes has been writing automobile history for more than four decades. A graduate of the University of Illinois and Penn State, she started her career at Automobile Quarterly in 1963. The author of countless automotive articles and books, she's won many awards for her work. A past president of the Society of Automotive Historians, Ms. Kimes has been the executive editor for the Classic Car Club of America since 1981.

Diana Meredith is a writer, interpreter and translator working in English, Spanish and French. She has traveled widely to research and uncover original sources and information related to the automotive industry with a focus on the period before World War II. A native of Chile, Ms. Meredith is based in Seattle, Washington.

Phil Patton is the author of many books on design and culture. He served as curatorial consultant for *Different Roads: Automobiles for the Next Century* at the Museum of Modern Art and other exhibitions. He writes on design for the *New York Times* and for many magazines and has appeared on a number of television series.

Automotive historian and writer **Jonathan A. Stein** is the Director of Publications for Hagerty Insurance. An automobile hobbyist for more than 30 years, Stein is best known for his work at *Automobile Quarterly* and extensive concours judging. His articles have appeared in numerous magazines and he is the author of two books: *British Sports Cars in America* and *The Performing Art of the American Automobile*. He resides in Reading, Pennsylvania.

Automotive designer and design educator **Geoff Wardle** studied at London's Royal College of Art. He has held both corporate and consulting positions with automakers, including British Leyland, Chrysler, PSA, International Automotive Design (IAD), SAAB Automobile, Ford Australia and Tatra. For the past decade he's been affiliated with the Art Center College of Design, first as Chair of Transportation Design (Swiss campus) and then as Corporate Relations Director and Transportation Design faculty in Pasadena.

ACKNOWLEDGEMENTS

A project of this scope and depth requires a significant group of talented professionals. Dedicated historians, writers, artists and researchers from around the United States and Europe, have contributed their time and energy in the pursuit of a superior exhibition and accompanying catalogue. Particular appreciation goes to those car owners who have lent to the exhibiton their extraordinary rolling works of art.

Those of us at Phoenix Museum of Art and Coachbuilt Press are forever indebted.

Car Owners
Bruce Barnett
Joseph Cassini III
Cavallino Holdings
William E. Connor, II
Gary Cullen
Arturo Keller
Sam Mann
J. Williard Marriott, Jr.
Bruce Meyer
Peter Mullin
James Patterson
Petersen Museum, Richard Messer
Ray Scherr
Larry Smith
Peter Williamson, MD

Car Logistics and Transportation
Carolyn Alley, Connors Collection
Lloyd Buck, Keller Collection
Pete Chapouris, SoCal Speed Shop
David Carte, Marriott Collection
Steven Costello, Cavallino Holdings
Thomas Kenney, Petersen Museum
Marci Marentette, General Motors
Alex Moldonado, SoCal Speed Shop
Jay Sanders, Art Center College of Design
Scott Sargent, Williamson Collection

Coachbuilt Press
Bill Beauchamp
Mary Dunham
Merrill Furman
Shelly Lesse
Phil Neff
David Phillips

Michael Furman Studio
Shawn Brackbill
Ken Burgess
Esteban Granados
Dave March
Dan Mezick
Jim Mital
Dan Murphy

Phoenix Museum of Art
Jim Ballinger
Kathryn Blake
Gene Koeneman
David Restad
Dennita Sewell
Lee Werhan
Ron Yagoda

Research
Michael Albano, General Motors
Stan Block
Lisa Bain, Daimler Chrysler
Richard Balsley, General Motors
Harold Dermott, McLaren Cars
Jerry Evans
Jennifer Flake, Ford Motor Company
David L. George II
Leslie Kendall, Petersen Museum
Michael Lamm
Michael Lynch
Byron Madsen, Cavallino Holdings
Carl Magnusson
J Mays, Ford Motor Company
Simon Moore
Doug Nye
Joe Richardson, Mercedes-Benz
Brandt Rosenbusch, Walter P. Chrysler Museum
Frederick A. Simeone, MD
Jim Sitz
Tom Tjaarda
James Wagner
Greg Wallace
Hampton Wayt
Ed Welburn, General Motors
Paul Wood

IMAGE CREDITS

Published by
Coachbuilt Press
Philadelphia, Pennsylvania
www.CoachbuiltPress.com

Published in conjunction with
Phoenix Art Museum
1625 N. Central Avenue
Phoenix, AZ 85004
www.PHXart.org

ISBN 978-0-9779809-2-5
Library of Congress Control Number: 2007923455

Photographs by Michael Furman made with PhaseOne digital capture on Sinar 4x5 and Hasselblad H1 cameras. Studio lighting by Broncolor. Photographs taken at Art Center College of Design, Pasedena, California and Hill Theatre Studio, Paulsboro, New Jersey. Digital imaging by David Phillips and Mary Dunham performed on Mac G5 computers running PhotoShop and CaptureOne software.

Exhibition Curator Dennita Sewell
Exhibition Designer David Restad
Illustrations by William Cauffiel Beauchamp
Manuscript edited by Merrill Furman
Typeset in Gill Sans and Gill Sans Light
Design by Mary Dunham, Coachbuilt Press

Printed by Mondadori Printing S.p.A., Verona, Italy

first edition